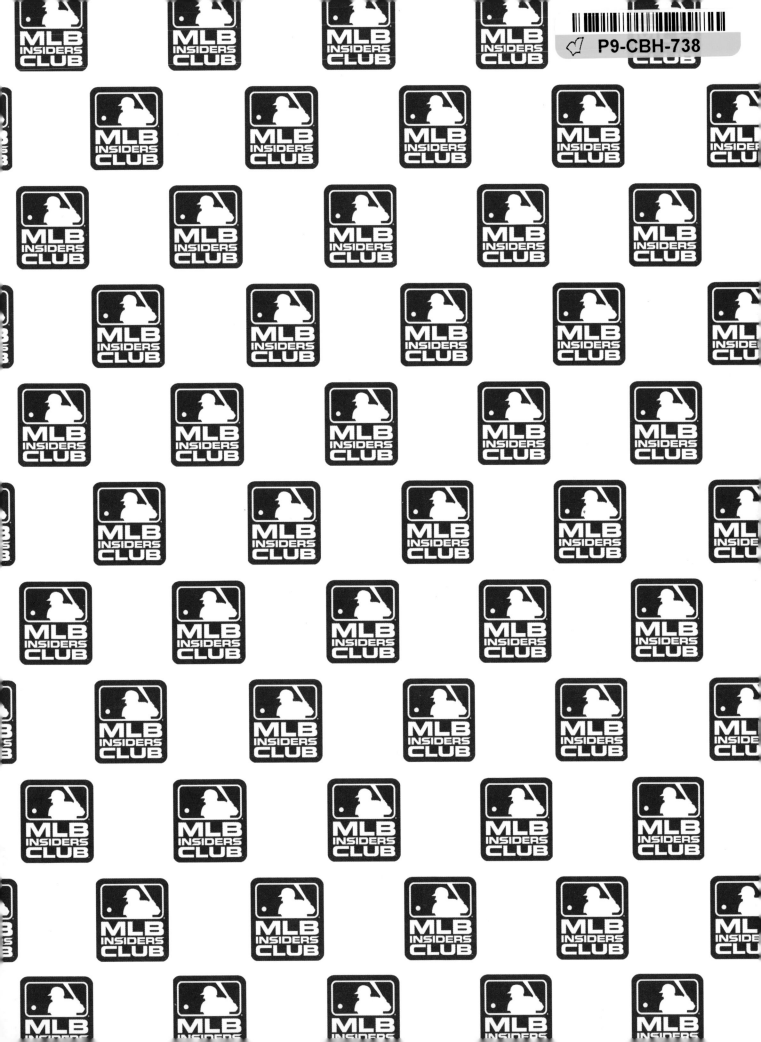

The Hall

A guided tour of the National Baseball Hall of Fame and Museum

The Hall

A guided tour of the National Baseball
Hall of Fame and Museum

MLB INSIDERS CLUB

Baseball Insiders Library

THE HALL by Bill Francis

A guided tour of the National Baseball Hall of Fame and Museum.

Printed in 2010

ABOUT THE AUTHOR

Bill Francis has worked at the National Baseball Hall of Fame and Museum since 1999, where he has contributed to the institution's yearbook, magazine and website. Prior to that, he served as a reporter and editor for a number of newspapers in Central New York. He lives in Cooperstown with his wife and two children.

ACKNOWLEDGEMENTS

Major League Baseball would like to offer thanks to all staff at the National Baseball Hall of Fame and Museum for being generous with their time and for sharing their unparalleled expertise on all matters relating to our national pastime. Special thanks go to Jeff Idelson, Brad Horn, Pat Kelly and Milo Stewart Jr. for their invaluable assistance; as well as Nathan Hale, Kristin Nieto and Eric Enders for their diligent work in helping to prepare this book for publication.

MAJOR LEAGUE BASEBALL PROPERTIES

Vice President, Publishing
Donald S. Hintze

Editorial Director
Mike McCormick

Publications Art Director
Faith M. Rittenberg

Senior Production Manager
Claire Walsh

Associate Editor
Jon Schwartz

Associate Art Director
Melanie Finnern

Senior Publishing Coordinator
Anamika Panchoo

Project Assistant Editors
Allison Duffy, Chris Greenberg, Jodie Jordan, Jake Schwartzstein

Editorial Interns
Daria Del Colliano, Harry Raymond

MAJOR LEAGUE BASEBALL PHOTOS

Director
Rich Pilling

Photo Editor
Jessica Foster

Photo Assistant
Kasey Cibrowski

MLB INSIDERS CLUB

Creative Director
Tom Carpenter

Managing Editor
Jen Weaverling

Prepress
Wendy Holdman

1 2 3 4 5 6 7 8 9 10 / 12 11 10

MLB Insiders Club
12301 Whitewater Drive
Minnetonka, MN 55343

Table of Contents

Introduction

Throughout the course of human history, men and women have journeyed to myriad sites of personal significance. They have forded treacherous rivers, crossed jagged mountains. These trips — usually long and arduous — ended at places that a person might feel compelled to see during their lifetime. Such destinations drew flocks because they may have been the final resting place of someone held in high esteem or because precious cultural relics could be visited. In the modern world, where technology has pulled the horizon closer and brought even the wonders of the ancient world into one's own home, there are few places that inspire such awe. For baseball fans, though, one such landmark still exists on the map. Devotees of the national pastime flock to Cooperstown, N.Y., to visit the National Baseball Hall of Fame and Museum.

Like so many hardball fans, veteran Big Leaguer Jim Thome planned a trip to the leafy village of Cooperstown, nestled in the heart of central New York's Leatherstocking region, with the person most responsible for imbuing in him a love for the game: his father, Chuck. After inclement weather twice thwarted their plans to travel to the Hall of Fame, the pair finally reached their destination on the third try. Not just the ultimate father-and-son dream, the adventure served another memorable purpose: The pair delivered the ball that the slugger hit for his 500th career home run on Sept. 16, 2007, while playing for the White Sox. For the younger Thome there was only one way to top the honor of becoming just the 23rd player in history to achieve the milestone.

"That one day of father-and-son enjoyment was important," Thome said. "Hopefully, I'll get to share it with my son and daughter someday and I can feel what my dad felt. To share it with my dad was a very special thing."

While a trip to the Hall of Fame may take on even greater meaning for a Big Leaguer, especially if he's arriving to donate a personal memento or, even better, to be enshrined as a Hall of Famer, this place strikes a chord with everyone who has ever swung a bat in a Little League contest or set foot in a ballpark. A shrine to the greatest players and a repository for the game's history, the National Baseball Hall of Fame and Museum elected its first class in 1936 — a prestigious group that included Babe Ruth, Ty Cobb, Walter Johnson, Honus Wagner and Christy Mathewson — and opened its doors on 25 Main Street in Cooperstown in 1939. Ever since, the Hall has been the conscience and memory of a game whose history stretches back deep into the 19th century.

With a vigilant staff keeping tabs on Major League milestones and historic moments, the Hall is always taking in new items to document the evolution of the game. Its collection has grown from an old baseball purchased by Cooperstown resident Stephen C. Clark, to more than 38,000 three-dimensional artifacts and innumerable other resources from photographs and press clippings to academic tools. Another invaluable method for filling the Hall's vault is soliciting donations from players like Thome. Of course, sometimes players need to experience Cooperstown for themselves before they understand the impact of sending items to the Hall. It was likely an encounter with "Black Betsy," the fabled bat that belonged to "Shoeless" Joe Jackson, that opened perennial All-Star Ichiro Suzuki's eyes to the magic of the Hall of Fame. After feeling the weight of Jackson's bat in his hands, on what became the first of many visits to the shrine, Ichiro became one of the institution's greatest champions.

"Once I experienced Cooperstown's magic firsthand and fully understood their mission, I regretted my reticence," Ichiro reflected. "Ever since, whenever they approach me for something, I'm honored to donate."

"The love for the game that motivated us once upon a time can get forgotten as baseball becomes an occupation," he said. "You would expect our affection for the game to grow as we live out our dreams on the field, but instead, we're pushed to focus on the occupational aspects. Cooperstown has a way of cleansing your heart. It allows you to rediscover the purity that originally attracted you to baseball. I feel that every time I visit, and that's what makes me want to return. It's a special place."

From profiles of the legendary ballplayers enshrined in the Hall of Fame's Plaque Gallery to in-depth excavations of the stories behind some of the most important artifacts housed in the Museum, *The Hall* offers readers the complete experience of a visit to Cooperstown. From the multimedia shows, the numerous exhibits, the vast resources of the Library, the annual events — headlined by the Induction Ceremony in July — that round out the Cooperstown calendar, everything that makes the National Baseball Hall of Fame and Museum one of the most special sites in the baseball landscape can be found on the behind-the-scenes tour filling the pages of this book.

The Doubleday Ball.

Chapter 1
The Plaque Gallery

"AS I LOOK AT THIS PLAQUE WITH MY LIKENESS, THIS HANDLEBAR MUSTACHE, I KNOW THAT 100 YEARS FROM NOW THERE WILL BE A 10-YEAR-OLD BOY THAT GOES UP TO HIS DAD AND SAYS, 'HEY DAD, THEY MESSED UP ON THIS. SHOULDN'T THIS SAY 1892 INSTEAD OF 1992?' I KNOW IT'S GOING TO HAPPEN."

ROLLIE FINGERS, AUG. 2, 1992

INDUCTION SPEECH

The Hall of Fame Plaques

No trip to the National Baseball Hall of Fame and Museum is complete without a walk through the Plaque Gallery. Exchanging wide-eyed glances and reverent whispers, visitors gaze upon the nearly 300 bronze tablets on the wall. Each plaque has a casting of the Hall of Famer at the top, as well as his name, teams he has played for and a biography, all written in raised block letters. Over the last few years, the responsibility of writing the biographies of the game's immortals has fallen on the shoulders of Hall of Fame Senior Director of Communications and Education, Brad Horn.

"We look at the totality of a player's career and try to incorporate all of the most important events, achievements, milestones," Horn says, "and have them fit into 90 words in a manner that is flattering toward the player and that provides insight and depth into his career.

"Not just the sense that they achieved statistical numbers, but how they achieved them. Was there a certain flair or panache or did they possess a certain level of respect among their peers?"

Horn's work begins shortly after any year's Hall of Fame election results are announced.

"It takes about three months in its entirety, so that we have written it and then rewritten, rewritten and rewritten to the point of satisfaction across several different layers of departments internally so that the final product is reflective, truly, of what an electee's career was."

And when the Commissioner of Baseball reads the plaque's text during the Induction Ceremony, it's also the first time the newest member of the game's most exclusive fraternity hears it.

Making a Hall of Fame Plaque

Along the walls inside the first floor Plaque Gallery at the National Baseball Hall of Fame and Museum reside nearly 300 bronze plaques with sculpted likenesses of the game's greatest figures. The labor-intensive plaque-creation process begins immediately after an election, when images are collected by the Hall of Fame and sent to Matthews International. The Pittsburgh bronze-casting firm has been in business since 1850 and its work can be seen at places ranging from the top of Pikes Peak in Colorado to Elvis Presley's grave. Matthews has been making plaques for the Baseball Hall of Fame since 1982. Each one currently costs approximately $2,000 to produce.

Even when inductees are still living, no personal sittings are needed since the plaques reflect what the individual looked like in the midst of his baseball career. Artists have photographs and video from the Hall's archives at their disposal as they endeavor to capture the essence of an individual in molding clay. With images in hand, artists like Mindy Ellis, who has been sculpting Hall of Fame plaques since 1995, can focus on each player's most recognizable facial features. While most of the likenesses are sculpted with a frontal view of the Hall of Famer's face, some — including Jack Chesbro, Yogi Berra, Tom Connolly, Charlie Gehringer, Harry Heilmann and Rogers Hornsby — are shown in profile. The bas relief faces are small, about four inches by three inches. The trick is to turn these two-dimensional images into a three-dimensional sculpture that juts out only about an inch.

"We select as wide a variety of images as we can, as well as video, so Mindy will have multiple poses, hairstyles, facial changes and so on," says Hall of Fame President, Jeff Idelson. "But we also select the one that we feel best represents that player from the era in which he dominated, and we ask Mindy to sculpt from that image." The Hall also determines which team cap will be depicted on a plaque. Despite the Hall's guidelines, there are quirky exceptions, such as Jim "Catfish" Hunter, pictured in a cap without a logo. There are also players with no cap: Jimmy Collins, Candy Cummings, Ed Delahanty, Hugh Duffy, Mike Kelly and, ironically, Cap Anson.

Once the clay mold is approved, it's set inside an aluminum frame that also includes the plaque's text. All this is then taken to the foundry, where a mold is created through a sandblasting process in which an impression is made in very fine, chemically treated sand. After the sand impression hardens, fiery molten bronze is poured into the mold.

When the metal hardens, it's removed from the mold, sandblasted, painted, buffed and highlighted, which brings out the natural color of the bronze. Finally, a clear protective coating is applied. In the end, the dimensions of each plaque are 15 1/2 inches high, 10 3/4 inches wide and 14 1/2 pounds in weight. With the process complete, the plaques are carefully packed, secured and hand-delivered to the Hall of Fame. Only one plaque per inductee is produced — although a miniature version is made for the inductee — and the mold used to create each plaque is destroyed when the process is complete. The result is a sculpted portrait and engaging text representative of the individual. The true test is seeing visitors just feet away from a favorite Hall of Famer's plaque, smiling and snapping photos.

Plaques from the Hall's gallery.

HENRY L. "HANK" AARON
MILWAUKEE N.L., ATLANTA N.L.,
MILWAUKEE A.L., 1954-1976
HIT 755 HOME RUNS IN 23-YEAR CAREER TO
BECOME MAJORS' ALL-TIME HOMER KING. HAD
20 OR MORE FOR 20 CONSECUTIVE YEARS, AT
LEAST 30 IN 15 SEASONS AND 40 OR BETTER
EIGHT TIMES. ALSO SET RECORD FOR GAMES
PLAYED (3,298), AT-BATS (12,364), LONG HITS
(1,477), TOTAL BASES (6,856), RUNS BATTED
IN (2,297). PACED N.L. IN BATTING TWICE
AND HOMERS, RUNS BATTED IN AND SLUGGING
PCT. FOUR TIMES EACH. WON MOST VALUABLE
PLAYER AWARD IN N.L. IN 1957.

ADRIAN CONSTANTINE ANSON
"CAP"
GREATEST HITTER AND GREATEST
NATIONAL LEAGUE PLAYER-MANAGER
OF 19TH CENTURY. STARTED WITH
CHICAGO IN NATIONAL LEAGUE'S
FIRST YEAR 1876. CHICAGO MANAGER
FROM 1879 TO 1897, WINNING 5 PENNANTS.
WAS .300 CLASS HITTER 20 YEARS,
BATTING CHAMPION 4 TIMES.

LUIS ERNESTO APARICIO
CHICAGO A.L. 1956-1962, 1968-1970
BALTIMORE A.L. 1963-1967
BOSTON A.L. 1971-1973
REGULAR SHORTSTOP FOR ALL OF HIS 18 SEASONS.
SET MAJOR CAREER RECORDS FOR MOST
GAMES (2,581), ASSISTS (8,016), CHANCES ACCEPTED
(12,564) AND DOUBLE PLAYS (1,553) BY A SHORTSTOP;
AND HAS MOST A.L. PUTOUTS (4,548). LED A.L. IN
FIELDING 8 TIMES. TOPPED LEAGUE IN STEALS
HIS FIRST 9 SEASONS, BEGINNING STOLEN BASE
RENAISSANCE. A.L. ROOKIE OF THE YEAR IN 1956

JAMES THOMAS BELL
"COOL PAPA"
NEGRO LEAGUES 1922-1950
COMBINED SPEED, DARING AND BATTING
SKILL TO RANK AMONG BEST PLAYERS
IN NEGRO LEAGUES. CONTEMPORARIES
RATED HIM FASTEST MAN ON BASE
PATHS. HIT OVER .300 REGULARLY,
TOPPING .400 ON OCCASION. PLAYED
29 SUMMERS AND 21 WINTERS
OF PROFESSIONAL BASEBALL.

JOHNNY LEE BENCH
CINCINNATI, N.L., 1967-1983
REDEFINED STANDARDS BY WHICH CATCHERS ARE
MEASURED DURING 17 SEASONS WITH "BIG RED MACHINE."
CONTROLLED GAME ON BOTH SIDES OF PLATE WITH
HIS HITTING (389 HOMERS-RECORD 327 AS A CATCHER,
1,376 RBI'S), THROWING OUT OPPOSING BASE RUNNERS,
CALLING PITCHES AND BLOCKING HOME PLATE. N.L.
MVP, 1970 AND 1972. WON 10 GOLD GLOVES. LAST GAME,
9TH INNING HOMER LED TO 1972 PENNANT.

LAWRENCE PETER BERRA
"YOGI"
NEW YORK, A.L. 1946-1963
NEW YORK, N.L. 1965
PLAYED ON MORE PENNANT-WINNERS (14) AND
WORLD CHAMPIONS (10) THAN ANY PLAYER IN
HISTORY. HAD 358 HOME RUNS AND LIFETIME
.285 BATTING AVERAGE. SET MANY RECORDS
FOR CATCHERS, INCLUDING 148 CONSECUTIVE
GAMES WITHOUT AN ERROR. VOTED A.L. MOST
VALUABLE PLAYER 1951-54-55. MANAGED
YANKEES TO PENNANT IN 1964.

WADE ANTHONY BOGGS
BOSTON, A.L. 1982-1992
NEW YORK, A.L. 1993-1997
TAMPA BAY, A.L. 1998-1999
A DISCIPLINED HITTER WHOSE COMMANDING KNOWLEDGE OF THE STRIKE ZONE
MADE HIM ONE OF BASEBALL'S TOUGHEST OUTS. ONLY 20TH CENTURY PLAYER
WITH SEVEN STRAIGHT 200-HIT SEASONS. REACHED BASE SAFELY IN 80 PERCENT
OF GAMES PLAYED. FIVE-TIME BATTING CHAMPION WHO VALUED THE LEAGUE IN ON-
BASE PERCENTAGE AND INTENTIONAL WALKS SIX TIMES EACH. A 12-TIME ALL-
STAR. HIT .328 WITH 3,010 HITS AND 1,412 WALKS. MEMBER OF THE 1996 WORLD
SERIES CHAMPION YANKEES AND WON TWO GOLD GLOVES. LEGENDARY FOR HIS
SUPERSTITIONS.

GEORGE HOWARD BRETT
KANSAS CITY, A.L. 1973-1993
PLAYED EACH GAME WITH FEARLESS INTENSITY AND UNBRIDLED
PASSION. CAREER MARKS INCLUDE .305 BATTING AVERAGE,
3,154 HITS, ELEVEN .300 SEASONS, A 10-TIME ALL-STAR. ONLY
FIRST PLAYER TO WIN BATTING TITLES IN THREE DECADES. A
POWER HITTER WITH 317 HOME RUNS AND 476 RBI IN 11 SEASONS THE
POWER-HITTING CHESTER CITIZEN MOVED IN THE RECORD BOOKS IN
.390. HIT .390 AND WAS NAMED A.L. MVP IN 1980. PLAYED IN SIX
WORLD SERIES TITLE IN 1985. LEADING ROYALS TO FIRST TITLE.
HITS, DOUBLES, LONG HITS AND 12-TIME ALL-STAR. SET A RECORD
MOST INTENTIONAL WALKS A.L. TEN SEASONS WITH .390 BATTING.
13 HITS ONE GAME AND FIVE HITS IN THREE DIFFERENT SERIES

ROBERTO CLEMENTE WALKER
PITTSBURGH N.L. 1955-1972
MEMBER OF EXCLUSIVE 3,000-HIT CLUB. LED
NATIONAL LEAGUE IN BATTING FOUR TIMES. HAD
FOUR SEASONS WITH 200 OR MORE HITS WHILE
POSTING LIFETIME .317 AVERAGE AND 240 HOME
RUNS. WON MOST VALUABLE PLAYER AWARD 1966.
RIFLE-ARMED DEFENSIVE STAR SET N.L. MARK BY
PACING OUTFIELDERS IN ASSISTS FIVE YEARS.
BATTED IN TWO WORLD SERIES, HITTING IN
ALL FOURTEEN GAMES

JOSEPH EDWARD CRONIN
PITTSBURGH N.L. 1926-1927
WASHINGTON A.L. 1928-1934
BOSTON A.L. 1935-1945
NAMED ALL-STAR SHORTSTOP SEVEN
SEASONS. MOST VALUABLE PLAYER A.L.
1930. LED A.L. SHORTSTOPS IN FIELDING
1931-1932. MOST PUTOUTS AND DOUBLE
PLAYS 1930-31-32. LIFETIME BATTING
AVERAGE .302. WON PENNANT IN 1933 IN
FIRST SEASON AS MANAGER WASHINGTON
A.L. AT AGE 26. TRADED TO BOSTON 1934 FOR
REPORTED RECORD PRICE OF $250,000.

JOSEPH PAUL DI MAGGIO
NEW YORK A.L. 1936 TO 1951
HIT SAFELY IN 56 CONSECUTIVE GAMES
FOR MAJOR LEAGUE RECORD 1941. HIT 2
HOME-RUNS IN ONE INNING 1936. HIT 3
HOME-RUNS IN ONE GAME (3 TIMES). HOLDS
NUMEROUS BATTING RECORDS. PLAYED IN
10 WORLD SERIES (51 GAMES) AND 11 ALL
STAR GAMES. MOST VALUABLE PLAYER
A.L. 1939, 1941, 1947.

LAWRENCE EUGENE DOBY
CLEVELAND, A.L. 1947-55, 1958
CHICAGO, A.L. 1956, 1959
DETROIT, A.L. 1959
EXCEPTIONAL ATHLETIC PROWESS AND A STAUNCH CONSTITUTION LED
TO A SUCCESSFUL PLAYING CAREER AFTER INTEGRATING THE
AMERICAN LEAGUE IN 1947. A SEVEN-TIME ALL-STAR WHO BATTED
WITH 253 HOME RUNS AND 970 RBI IN 13 MAJOR LEAGUE SEASONS. THE
POWER-HITTING CENTER FIELDER PACED THE A.L. IN HOME RUNS
TWICE AND COLLECTED 100 RBI FIVE TIMES. WHILE LEADING THE
INDIANS TO PENNANTS IN 1948 AND 1954. APPOINTED MANAGER OF THE
WHITE SOX IN 1978. THE SECOND AFRO-AMERICAN TO LEAD A
MAJOR LEAGUE CLUB. PLAYED FOUR SEASONS WITH NEWARK IN THE
NEGRO NATIONAL LEAGUE FOLLOWING PLAYER CAREER WORKED AS A
SCOUT AND MAJOR LEAGUE BASEBALL EXECUTIVE

DONALD SCOTT DRYSDALE
BROOKLYN N.L. 1956-1957
LOS ANGELES N.L. 1958-1969
HARD-THROWING SIDE-ARMER NOTED FOR
INTIMIDATING STYLE AND DURABILITY. HAD 209-166
RECORD WITH 2.95 ERA AND 2,486 STRIKEOUTS.
LED N.L. IN STRIKEOUTS 3 TIMES AND HURLED 49
SHUTOUTS. WAS 25-9 IN 1962 AND WON CY YOUNG
AWARD. THREW 6 SHUTOUTS IN A ROW IN 1968,
SETTING RECORD WITH 58 CONSECUTIVE SCORELESS
INNINGS. PITCHED IN RECORD 8 ALL-STAR GAMES.

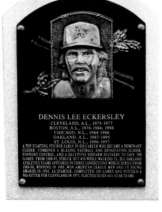

DENNIS LEE ECKERSLEY
CLEVELAND, A.L., 1975-1977
BOSTON, A.L., 1978-1984, 1998
CHICAGO, N.L., 1984-1986
OAKLAND, A.L., 1987-1995
ST. LOUIS, N.L., 1996-1997
A TOP STARTING PITCHER EARLY IN HIS CAREER WHO BECAME A DOMINANT
CLOSER. COMBINED A BLAZING FASTBALL AND DEVASTATING SLIDER,
PINPOINT CONTROL, AND A DECEPTIVE SIDEARM DELIVERY TO SAVE 390
GAMES. FROM 1988-92, STRUCK OUT 458 WHILE WALKING 51. HIS OAKLAND
ATHLETICS TEAMS APPEARED IN THREE CONSECUTIVE WORLD SERIES FROM
1988-90, WINNING IN 1989. WON AMERICAN LEAGUE MVP AND CY YOUNG
AWARDS IN 1992 AS STARTER, COMPLETED 100 GAMES AND PITCHED A
NO-HITTER FOR CLEVELAND IN 1977. ELECTED TO SIX ALL-STAR TEAMS.

ROBERT WILLIAM ANDREW FELLER
CLEVELAND A.L. 1936 TO 1941
1945 TO 1956
PITCHED 3 NO-HIT GAMES IN A.L. 12 ONE-HIT GAMES.
SET MODERN STRIKEOUT RECORD WITH 18 IN GAME,
348 FOR SEASON. LED A.L. IN VICTORIES 6 (ONE TIE)
SEASONS. LIFETIME RECORD WON 266, LOST 162, PC
.621. E.R. AVERAGE 3.25, STRUCKOUT 2581.

JAMES E. (JIMMY) FOXX
PHILADELPHIA (A.L.) 1926-35
BOSTON (A.L.) 1936-42; CHICAGO (N.L.) 1942-44
PHILADELPHIA (N.L.) 1945
NOTED FOR HIS BATTING, PARTICULARLY AS A
HOME RUN HITTER. COLLECTED 534 HOME RUNS
IN 2,317 GAMES. HAD A LIFETIME BATTING
AVERAGE OF .325 AND IN THREE WORLD
SERIES, COMPILED A MARK OF .344. APPEARED
IN SEVEN ALL-STAR GAMES IN WHICH HE
BATTED .316. PLAYED FIRST AND THIRD BASES
AND ALSO WAS A CATCHER.

JOSHUA (JOSH) GIBSON
NEGRO LEAGUES 1930·1946
CONSIDERED GREATEST SLUGGER IN NEGRO
BASEBALL LEAGUES. POWER-HITTING CATCHER
WHO HIT ALMOST 800 HOME RUNS IN LEAGUE
AND INDEPENDENT BASEBALL DURING HIS
17-YEAR CAREER. CREDITED WITH HAVING
BEEN NEGRO NATIONAL LEAGUE BATTING
CHAMPION IN 1936·38·42·43.

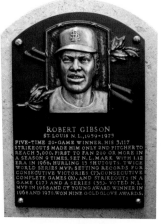

ROBERT GIBSON
ST. LOUIS N.L.,1959·1975
FIVE-TIME 20-GAME WINNER. HIS 3,117
STRIKEOUTS MADE HIM ONLY 2ND PITCHER TO
REACH 3,000. FIRST TO FAN 200 OR MORE IN
A SEASON 9 TIMES. SET N.L.MARK WITH 1.12
ERA IN 1968, HURLING 13 SHUTOUTS. TWICE
WORLD SERIES MVP, SETTING RECORDS FOR
CONSECUTIVE VICTORIES (7), CONSECUTIVE
COMPLETE GAMES (8), AND STRIKEOUTS IN A
GAME (17) AND A SERIES (35). VOTED N.L.
MVP IN 1968 AND CY YOUNG AWARD WINNER IN
1968 AND 1970. WON NINE GOLD GLOVE AWARDS.

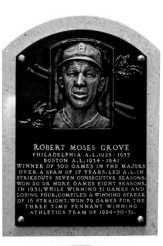

ROBERT MOSES GROVE
PHILADELPHIA A.L.1925·1933
BOSTON A.L.1934·1941
WINNER OF 300 GAMES IN THE MAJORS
OVER A SPAN OF 17 YEARS. LED A.L. IN
STRIKEOUTS SEVEN CONSECUTIVE SEASONS.
WON 20 OR MORE GAMES EIGHT SEASONS.
IN 1931, WHILE WINNING 31 GAMES AND
LOSING FOUR, COMPILED A WINNING STREAK
OF 16 STRAIGHT. WON 79 GAMES FOR THE
THREE TIME PENNANT WINNING
ATHLETICS TEAM OF 1929·30·31.

CARL HUBBELL
NEW YORK N.L.1928·1943
HAILED FOR IMPRESSIVE PERFORMANCE IN
1934 ALL-STAR GAME WHEN HE STRUCK OUT
RUTH, GEHRIG, FOXX, SIMMONS AND CRONIN
IN SUCCESSION. NICKNAMED GIANTS'
MEAL-TICKET. WON 253 GAMES IN MAJORS,
SCORING 16 STRAIGHT IN 1936. COMPILED
STREAK OF 46⅓ SCORELESS INNINGS IN
1933. HOLDER OF MANY RECORDS.

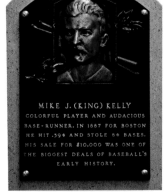

MIKE J. (KING) KELLY
COLORFUL PLAYER AND AUDACIOUS
BASE-RUNNER. IN 1887 FOR BOSTON
HE HIT .394 AND STOLE 84 BASES.
HIS SALE FOR $10,000 WAS ONE OF
THE BIGGEST DEALS OF BASEBALL'S
EARLY HISTORY.

HARMON CLAYTON KILLEBREW
WASHINGTON A.L. 1954·1960
MINNESOTA A.L. 1961·1974
KANSAS CITY A.L. 1975
MUSCULAR SLUGGER WITH MONUMENTAL HOME
RUN AND RBI SUCCESS. HIS 573 HOMERS OVER
22 YEARS RANK FIFTH ALL-TIME AND SECOND
ONLY TO RUTH AMONG A.L. HITTERS. TIED OR
LED A.L. IN HOME RUNS 6 TIMES. BELTED OVER
40 ON 8 OCCASIONS AND IS THIRD IN HOME RUN
FREQUENCY. DROVE IN OVER 100 RUNS 9 TIMES.
A.L. MVP IN 1969.

NAPOLEON (LARRY) LAJOIE
PHILADELPHIA (N) 1896·1900
PHILADELPHIA (A) 1901
CLEVELAND (A) 1902·14
PHILADELPHIA (A) 1915·16
GREAT HITTER AND MOST GRACEFUL
AND EFFECTIVE SECOND·BASEMAN
OF HIS ERA. MANAGED CLEVELAND 4
YEARS. LEAGUE BATTING CHAMPION
1901·03·04.

WALTER FENNER LEONARD
"BUCK"
NEGRO LEAGUES 1933·1950
FIRST BASEMAN OF HOMESTEAD GRAYS WHEN
TEAM WON NEGRO NATIONAL LEAGUE PENNANT
NINE YEARS IN A ROW 1937·1945. TEAMED
WITH JOSH GIBSON TO FORM MOST FEARED
BATTING TWOSOME IN NEGRO BASEBALL FROM
1937 TO 1946. RANKED AMONG NEGRO HOME
RUN LEADERS. WON NEGRO NATIONAL LEAGUE
BATTING TITLE WITH 391 AVERAGE IN 1948.

**JUAN ANTONIO
MARICHAL SANCHEZ**
SAN FRANCISCO N.L. 1960·1973 BOSTON A.L. 1974
LOS ANGELES N.L. 1975
HIGH-KICKING RIGHT-HANDER FROM DOMINICAN
REPUBLIC. WON 243 GAMES AND LOST ONLY 142
OVER 16 SEASONS. WON 20 GAMES SIX TIMES AND
NO-HIT HOUSTON IN 1963. LED N.L. IN COMPLETE
GAMES AND SHUTOUTS TWICE AND IN ERA WITH
2.10 IN 1969. COMPLETED 244 GAMES DURING
CAREER, STRIKING OUT 2,303 AND FINISHING
WITH 2.89 ERA.

EDWIN LEE MATHEWS
BOSTON N.L., MILWAUKEE N.L.,
ATLANTA N.L., HOUSTON N.L.,
DETROIT A.L. 1952·1968
BECAME SEVENTH PLAYER IN MAJOR LEAGUE
HISTORY TO HIT 500 HOME RUNS. FINISHED
CAREER WITH 512. HIT 30 OR MORE HOMERS
NINE YEARS IN ROW, 1953·1961, REACHING
40 MARK FOUR TIMES. ESTABLISHED RECORD
FOR HOMERS IN SEASON BY THIRD BASEMAN
WITH 47 IN 1953. LED N.L. IN HOME RUNS
TWICE AND IN WALKS FOUR TIMES. HAD FIVE
SEASONS OF 100 OR MORE RUNS BATTED IN.

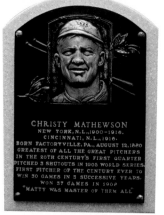

CHRISTY MATHEWSON
NEW YORK, N.L., 1900·1916.
CINCINNATI, N.L., 1916.
BORN FACTORYVILLE, PA., AUGUST 12, 1880.
GREATEST OF ALL THE GREAT PITCHERS
IN THE 20TH CENTURY'S FIRST QUARTER.
PITCHED 3 SHUTOUTS IN 1905 WORLD SERIES.
FIRST PITCHER OF THE CENTURY EVER TO
WIN 30 GAMES IN 3 SUCCESSIVE YEARS.
WON 37 GAMES IN 1908.
"MATTY WAS MASTER OF THEM ALL"

WILLIAM STANLEY MAZEROSKI
"MAZ"
PITTSBURGH N.L. 1956·1972
A DEFENSIVE WIZARD WHOSE HARD-NOSED HUSTLE AND QUIET WORK
ETHIC HELPED LEAD THE PIRATES TO THREE DIVISION TITLES,
TWO PENNANTS AND A PAIR OF WORLD SERIES CHAMPIONSHIPS. AN
EIGHT-TIME GOLD GLOVE WINNER AND 10-TIME ALL-STAR
RENOWNED FOR HIS LIGHTNING-QUICK PIVOT ON THE DOUBLE PLAY.
TURNING 100 OR MORE IN 11 CONSECUTIVE YEARS. HIS 1,706 CAREER
TWIN KILLINGS IS A RECORD AMONG MIDDLE INFIELDERS. ALSO RANKS
IN THE TOP 10 AMONG SECOND BASEMEN IN ASSISTS, PUTOUTS AND
GAMES PLAYED. HIS DRAMATIC HOME RUN IN GAME SEVEN AT FORBES
FIELD PROPELLED THE PIRATES TO THE 1960 WORLD CHAMPIONSHIP.

WILLIE LEE McCOVEY
"STRETCH"
SAN FRANCISCO, N.L., 1959·1973, 1977·1980
SAN DIEGO, N.L., 1974·1976
OAKLAND, A.L., 1976
TOP LEFT-HANDED HOME RUN HITTER IN N.L.
HISTORY WITH 521. SECOND ONLY TO LOU GEHRIG
WITH 18 CAREER GRAND SLAMS. LED N.L. IN HOMERS
THREE TIMES AND IN R.B.I. TWICE. N.L. ROOKIE OF
YEAR IN 1959. MVP IN 1969 AND COMEBACK PLAYER
OF THE YEAR IN '77. TEAMED WITH WILLIE MAYS
FOR AWESOME 1-2 PUNCH IN GIANTS' LINEUP.

JOSÉ DE LA CARIDAD MÉNDEZ BAEZ
"EL DIAMANTE NEGRO" "THE BLACK DIAMOND"
PRE-NEGRO LEAGUES, 1908·1919
NEGRO LEAGUES, 1920·1926
A SLENDER RIGHT-HANDED PITCHER WHO WAS ACKNOWLEDGED AS THE
FIRST CUBAN RIGHT BASEBALL STAR IN THE PRE-NEGRO LEAGUES ERA.
UTILIZED A VAST ARRAY OF PITCHES, MAINLY RELYING ON A DECEPTIVE
FASTBALL AND SHARP-BREAKING CURVE TO DOMINATE OPPOSING
BATTERS AS PLAYER-MANAGER, LED KANSAS CITY MONARCHS TO
THREE CONSECUTIVE NEGRO NATIONAL LEAGUE PENNANTS, 1923·1925.
CLINCHED 1924 NEGRO LEAGUES WORLD SERIES TITLE WITH THREE-HIT
SHUTOUT. HURLED 25 CONSECUTIVE SHUTOUT INNINGS AGAINST THE
CINCINNATI REDS DURING EXHIBITION COMPETITION IN 1908.

MELVIN T. (MEL) OTT
NEW YORK (N.L.) 1926·48
ONE OF FEW PLAYERS TO JUMP FROM A HIGH
SCHOOL TEAM TO MAJORS. PLAYED OUTFIELD
AND THIRD BASE AND MANAGED CLUB FROM
DEC. 1941 THROUGH JULY 1948. HIT 511 HOME
RUNS, N.L. RECORD WHEN HE RETIRED. ALSO
LED IN MOST RUNS SCORED, MOST RUNS BATTED
IN, TOTAL BASES, BASES ON BALLS AND EXTRA
BASES ON LONG HITS. HAD A .304 LIFETIME
BATTING AVERAGE. PLAYED IN ELEVEN ALL STAR
GAMES AND IN THREE WORLD SERIES.

LEROY ROBERT PAIGE
"SATCHEL"
NEGRO LEAGUES   1926·1947
CLEVELAND A.L.   1948·1949
ST. LOUIS A.L.   1951·1953
KANSAS CITY A.L.   1965
PAIGE WAS ONE OF THE GREATEST STARS
TO PLAY IN THE NEGRO BASEBALL LEAGUES.
THRILLED MILLIONS OF PEOPLE AND WON
HUNDREDS OF GAMES. STRUCK OUT 21 MAJOR
LEAGUERS IN AN EXHIBITION GAME. HELPED
PITCH CLEVELAND INDIANS TO THE 1948
PENNANT IN HIS FIRST BIG LEAGUE YEAR
AT AGE 42. HIS PITCHING WAS A LEGEND
AMONG MAJOR LEAGUE HITTERS.

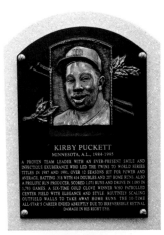

KIRBY PUCKETT
MINNESOTA, A.L., 1984-1995
A PROVEN TEAM LEADER WITH AN EVER-PRESENT SMILE AND
INFECTIOUS EXUBERANCE WHO LED THE TWINS TO WORLD SERIES
TITLES IN 1987 AND 1991. OVER 12 SEASONS HIT FOR POWER AND
AVERAGE, BATTING .318 WITH 414 DOUBLES AND 207 HOME RUNS. ALSO
A PROLIFIC RUN PRODUCER, SCORED 1,071 RUNS AND DROVE IN 1,085 IN
1,783 GAMES. A SIX-TIME GOLD GLOVE WINNER WHO PATROLLED
CENTER FIELD WITH ELEGANCE AND STYLE ROUTINELY SCALING
OUTFIELD WALLS TO TAKE AWAY HOME RUNS. THE 10-TIME
ALL-STAR'S CAREER ENDED ABRUPTLY DUE TO IRREVERSIBLE RETINAL
DAMAGE IN HIS RIGHT EYE.

CHARLIE RADBOURNE
"OLD HOSS"
PROVIDENCE, BOSTON AND CINCINNATI
NATIONAL LEAGUE 1881 TO 1891. GREATEST
OF ALL 19TH CENTURY PITCHERS. WINNING
1884 PENNANT FOR PROVIDENCE, RADBOURNE
PITCHED LAST 27 GAMES OF SEASON, WON
26. WON 3 STRAIGHT IN WORLD SERIES.

HAROLD HENRY "PEE WEE" REESE
BROOKLYN N.L. 1940-1957
LOS ANGELES N.L. 1958
SHORTSTOP AND CAPTAIN OF GREAT DODGER TEAMS
OF 1940'S AND 50'S. INTANGIBLE QUALITIES OF SUBTLE
LEADERSHIP AND OFF FIELD, COMPETITIVE FIRE
AND PROFESSIONAL PRIDE COMPLEMENTED DEPENDABLE
GLOVE, RELIABLE BASE-RUNNING AND CLUTCH-HITTING
AS SIGNIFICANT FACTORS IN 7 DODGER PENNANTS.
INSTRUMENTAL IN EASING ACCEPTANCE OF JACKIE
ROBINSON AS BASEBALL'S FIRST BLACK PERFORMER.

BROOKS CALBERT ROBINSON, JR.
BALTIMORE A.L. 1955-1977
ESTABLISHED MODERN STANDARD OF EXCELLENCE
FOR THIRD BASEMEN, SETTING MAJOR LEAGUE
RECORDS AT HIS POSITION FOR SEASONS (23),
FIELDING PCT. (.971), GAMES (2,870), PUTOUTS
(2,697), ASSISTS (6,205), AND DOUBLE PLAYS (618).
HIT 268 CAREER HOME RUNS. NAMED TO 18
CONSECUTIVE ALL-STAR TEAMS. MVP OF 1970
WORLD SERIES. AMERICAN LEAGUE MVP IN 1964.

AMOS WILSON RUSIE
"THE HOOSIER THUNDERBOLT"
INDIANAPOLIS N.L., NEW YORK N.L.
1889-1895
1897-1898 AND 1901
GENERALLY CONSIDERED FIREBALL KING OF
NINETEENTH-CENTURY MOUNDSMEN. NOTCHED
BETTER THAN 240 VICTORIES IN TEN-YEAR
CAREER. ACHIEVED 30-VICTORY MARK FOUR
YEARS IN A ROW AND WON 20 OR MORE GAMES
EIGHT SUCCESSIVE TIMES. LED LEAGUE IN
STRIKEOUTS FIVE YEARS AND LED OR TIED
FOR MOST SHUTOUTS FIVE TIMES.

RYNE DEE SANDBERG
"RYNO"
PHILADELPHIA, N.L. 1981
CHICAGO, N.L. 1982-1994, 1996-1997
A SURE-HANDED SECOND BASEMAN WITH POWER AND SPEED WHO
DIGNIFIED THE GAME WITH HIS PROFESSIONALISM, QUIET LEADERSHIP
AND TIRELESS PREPARATION. SET CAREER RECORDS AMONG SECOND
BASEMEN FOR HOME RUNS (277 OF 282 OVERALL), FIELDING
PERCENTAGE (.989), CONSECUTIVE ERRORLESS GAMES IN A ROW (123)
AND OVER TWO SEASONS (123). EARNED NINE GOLD GLOVES, LED
LEAGUE IN RUNS SCORED THREE TIMES. ELECTED TO 10 ALL-STAR
TEAMS, AND NAMED NATIONAL LEAGUE MVP IN 1984. HELPED TIE CUBS
TO TWO DIVISION TITLES, HITTING .385 IN 10 POST-SEASON GAMES.

GEORGE HAROLD SISLER
ST. LOUIS - WASHINGTON A.L.
BOSTON, N.L. 1915-1930
HOLDS TWO AMERICAN LEAGUE RECORDS,
MAKING 257 HITS IN 1920 AND BATTING
.41970 IN 1922. RETIRED WITH MAJOR
LEAGUE AVERAGE OF .341. CREDITED WITH
BEING ONE OF BEST TWO FIELDING FIRST
BASEMEN IN HISTORY OF GAME.

WARREN EDWARD SPAHN
BOSTON N.L., MILWAUKEE N.L.,
NEW YORK N.L., SAN FRANCISCO N.L.,
1942-1965
BECAME FIFTH BIGGEST WINNER IN MAJORS'
HISTORY WITH 363 VICTORIES. MOST
VICTORIES FOR A LEFT-HANDER. WON 20
OR MORE GAMES 13 SEASONS, SIX IN A ROW.
SET ALL-TIME RECORDS FOR YEARS LEADING
LEAGUE IN VICTORIES (8) AND COMPLETE
GAMES (9). ALSO N.L. CAREER HIGHS WITH
665 GAMES STARTED; 5,264 INNINGS;
2,583 STRIKEOUTS. PITCHED NO-HITTER
IN 1960, ANOTHER IN 1961.

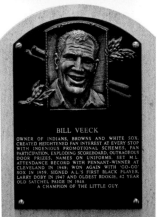

BILL VEECK
OWNER OF INDIANS, BROWNS AND WHITE SOX.
CREATED HEIGHTENED FAN INTEREST AT EVERY STOP
WITH INGENIOUS PROMOTIONAL SCHEMES, FAN
PARTICIPATION, EXPLODING SCOREBOARD, OUTRAGEOUS
DOOR PRIZES, NAMES ON UNIFORMS. SET M.L.
ATTENDANCE RECORD WITH PENNANT-WINNER AT
CLEVELAND IN 1948; WON AGAIN WITH "GO-GO
SOX IN 1959. SIGNED A.L.'S FIRST BLACK PLAYER,
LARRY DOBY IN 1947 AND OLDEST ROOKIE, 42 YEAR
OLD SATCHEL PAIGE IN 1948.
A CHAMPION OF THE LITTLE GUY.

WILVER DORNEL STARGELL
"WILLIE"
PITTSBURGH, N.L. 1962-1982
INTIMIDATING PRESENCE BETWEEN THE LINES
AND CHARISMATIC PATRIARCH IN CLUBHOUSE
AND DUGOUT. CRUSHED 475 HOMERS, MANY
OF TAPE-MEASURE VARIETY AND HIT MOST
BY ANY PLAYER DURING 1970'S. LIKE HIS
ROUND-TRIPPERS. HIS 1,540 RBIS ALSO MOST
EVER BY A PIRATE. BATTED .282 OVER 21
SEASONS, ALL WITH PITTSBURGH. SHARED N.L.
MVP HONORS IN 1979, AND NAMED MVP IN '79
N.L. CHAMPIONSHIP SERIES AND WORLD SERIES.

CHARLES DILLON STENGEL
"CASEY"
MANAGED NEW YORK YANKEES 1949-1960.
WON 10 PENNANTS AND 7 WORLD SERIES WITH
NEW YORK YANKEES. ONLY MANAGER TO WIN
5 CONSECUTIVE WORLD SERIES 1949-1953.
PLAYED OUTFIELD 1912-1925 WITH BROOKLYN,
PITTSBURGH, PHILADELPHIA, NEW YORK AND
BOSTON N.L. TEAMS. MANAGED BROOKLYN
1934-1936, BOSTON BRAVES 1938-1943,
NEW YORK METS 1962-1965.

JOSEPH B. TINKER
FAMOUS AS A MEMBER OF ONE OF BASEBALL'S
GREATEST DOUBLE PLAY COMBINATIONS-FROM
TINKER TO EVERS TO CHANCE. A BIG LEAGUER
FROM 1902 THROUGH 1916 WITH THE CHICAGO
CUBS AND CINCINNATI REDS AND THE
CHICAGO FEDS. MANAGER CINCINNATI
1913 AND CHICAGO N.L. 1916. SHORTSTOP
ON CUBS' TEAM THAT WON PENNANTS
IN 1906,'07 '08 AND 1910.

ARTHUR CHARLES (DAZZY) VANCE
BROOKLYN N.L. 1922 TO 1932, 1935
PITTSBURGH N.L. • NEW YORK A.L.
ST. LOUIS N.L. - CINCINNATI N.L.

FIRST PITCHER IN N.L. TO LEAD IN
STRIKEOUTS FOR 7 STRAIGHT YEARS, 1922 TO
1928. LED LEAGUE WITH 28 VICTORIES IN
1924; 22 IN 1925. WON 15 STRAIGHT IN 1924.
PITCHED NO-HIT GAME AGAINST PHILLIES,
1925. MOST VALUABLE PLAYER N.L. 1924.

HONUS WAGNER
LOUISVILLE, N.L. 1897-1899.
PITTSBURGH, N.L. 1900-1917.
THE GREATEST SHORTSTOP IN BASEBALL
HISTORY. BORN CARNEGIE, PA., FEB. 24, 1874
KNOWN TO FAME AS "HONUS", "HANS"
AND "THE FLYING DUTCHMAN" RETIRED IN 1917,
HAVING SCORED MORE RUNS, MADE MORE
HITS AND STOLEN MORE BASES THAN
ANY OTHER PLAYER IN THE HISTORY
OF HIS LEAGUE.

EARL SIDNEY WEAVER
BALTIMORE, A.L. 1968-1982, 1985-1986
MANAGED ORIOLES WITH INTENSITY, FLAIR AND
ACERBIC WIT FOR 17 SEASONS. .583 WINNING
PERCENTAGE (.1480-1060). RANKS FIFTH ALL-TIME
AMONG 20TH CENTURY MANAGERS WITH 10 OR MORE
YEARS SERVICE. 94.3 WINS PER SEASON RANKS FIRST
FIVE .100 WIN SEASONS SECOND ON ALL-TIME LIST.
WON SIX A.L. EAST TITLES, FOUR PENNANTS AND 1970
WORLD SERIES.

CARL MICHAEL YASTRZEMSKI
"YAZ"
BOSTON, A.L. 1961-1983
SUCCEEDED TED WILLIAMS IN FENWAY'S LEFT FIELD
IN 1961 AND RETIRED 23 YEARS LATER AS ALL-TIME
RED SOX LEADER IN 8 CATEGORIES. PLAYED WITH
GRACEFUL INTENSITY IN RECORD 3,308 A.L. GAMES.
ONLY A.L. PLAYER WITH 3,000 HITS AND 400 HOMERS.
7-TIME BATTING CHAMPION. WON MVP AND TRIPLE
CROWN IN 1967 AS HE LED RED SOX TO IMPOSSIBLE
DREAM PENNANT.

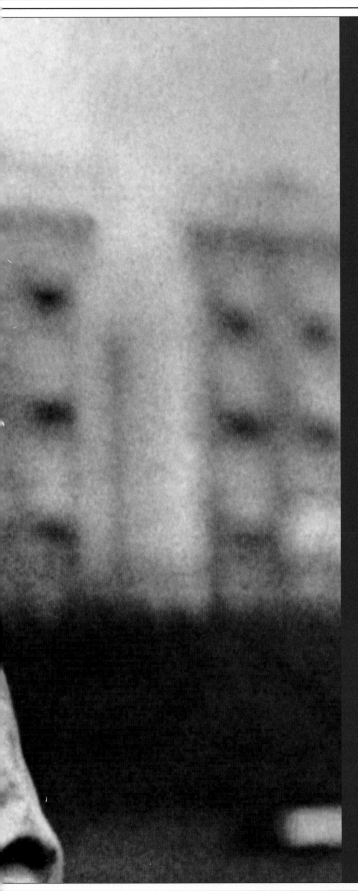

CY YOUNG

INDUCTED IN 1939

IN 1892, IN just his third year playing in the National League, Cy Young collected a career-high 36 wins, making up more than one third of his team's 93 victories that season. To get to that number, he started 49 games and tossed 453 innings for the National League's Cleveland Spiders — numbers that seem nearly impossible to believe compared to modern day performances. And the following year, Young nearly matched them, proceeding to win a whopping 34 contests in a total of 46 starts. Of those, 42 were complete-game outings.

Over the course of the next 18 Major League seasons, Young would frequently challenge those marks, crossing the 30-win plateau on three additional occasions. It was a remarkable display of stamina that not only placed him at the top of many of the game's all-time lists, but also cemented his legend in baseball as one of the best hurlers of all time. All told, Young won 511 career games, nearly 100 more than runner-up Walter Johnson. He threw a record 7,356 innings — more than Sandy Koufax, Pedro Martinez and Mariano Rivera combined.

Comparing Young's career statistics to the other greats of his day, and even stars of more modern eras, makes it clear how much of a workhorse he was. He is appropriately the namesake of the Cy Young Award, given annually to the best pitcher in each league.

Chapter 2
Induction

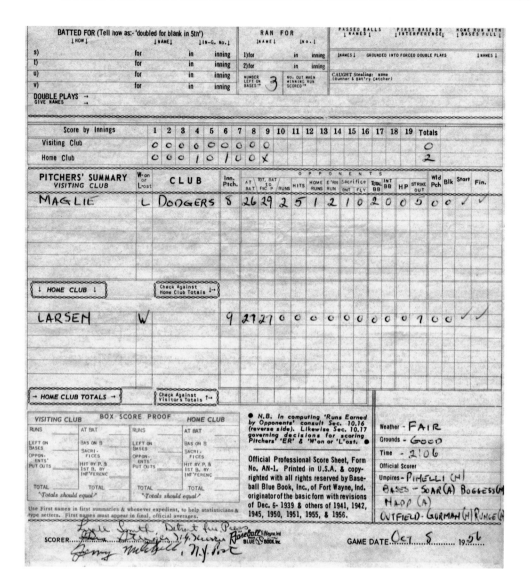

As he took the mound on Oct. 8, 1956, Don Larsen was just about the last person expected to pitch the first World Series perfect game. He had a career record of 30-40, went 3-21 in 1954 and had pitched poorly in Game 2. When he arrived at Yankee Stadium before Game 5, Larsen was shocked to see a baseball in his shoe — pitching coach Jim Turner's way of giving him the nod.

After sleeping off a long night in the trainer's room, Larsen took the mound feeling refreshed. A wild pitcher, he had walked 96 men during the regular season and four more in Game 2. But that day, his no-windup delivery — adopted just two weeks prior — was working to perfection.

For nine innings Larsen dominated a Dodgers lineup that included Duke Snider, Roy Campanella and Jackie Robinson. Larsen had luck on his side, too. In the fifth, Mickey Mantle made an outstanding catch and Sandy Amoros hit a no-doubt homer that was called foul.

After that, the perfect game seemed inevitable. Larsen ended matters by striking out Dale Mitchell looking on a disputed call with two outs in the ninth, and famously caught a leaping Yogi Berra in celebration. The game's score sheet is part of the Hall's collections and pictured above.

The Vote

MANY OF THOSE ENSHRINED IN THE NATIONAL BASEBALL HALL OF Fame have been elected by the Baseball Writers' Association of America (BBWAA), an organization founded in 1908 to improve working conditions for journalists in the early 20th century.

When the notion of the Baseball Hall of Fame was still in its embryonic stages during the mid-1930s, it was decided that "modern" players would be voted on by members of the BBWAA. Players would be required to receive votes on 75 percent of the ballots cast in order to gain induction to the Hall.

But unlike today, in those first years the rules for election by the BBWAA were less structured. With no guidelines on who was eligible, it was merely assumed that BBWAA members would vote for contemporary players from the 20th century.

In 1946, it was decided that a player had to be retired for a full year in order to be eligible for election, but by 1954 a five-year waiting period went into effect, and is still used today.

The BBWAA restricted voting to 10-year members in 1947 and has held a Hall of Fame election every year since 1966. The first 30 years of voting sometimes saw one or two years between votes, and there have been nine occasions when no election was held.

Now in its more rigidly structured form, anticipation grows every winter when the BBWAA results are ready to be announced. Approximately 500 members vote in any given year — at least 400 ballots have been cast in every election since 1986 — and voters can select up to 10 names on their ballot.

The most candidates elected by the BBWAA in a year was five, and that came in 1936, the very first election. The names chosen that year were legendary: Babe Ruth, Ty Cobb, Walter Johnson, Honus Wagner and Christy Mathewson. On the other extreme, seven elections have seen no players earn enough votes for induction. The length of time a player remains on the BBWAA ballot has varied throughout the Hall of Fame's history. From 1946–56, it was required that a player have been active at some point in the 25 years prior to the election; it was increased to 30 years from 1956–62, and has been 20 ever since.

No individual has been elected unanimously to the Hall of Fame, but there have been close calls. Topping the list is Tom Seaver, elected in 1992 when he received votes on 98.84 percent (425 of 430) of the ballots cast. One of Seaver's former teammates with the New York Mets, Nolan Ryan, is next with his 98.79 percent (491 of 497) in 1999, while Cal Ripken Jr. is third with 98.53 percent (537 of 545) in 2007.

Rules for Election

CERTAINLY A PLAYER WITH 3,000 HITS GETS A BRONZE PLAQUE IN Cooperstown, right? A hurler with 300 wins? A manager with multiple World Series crowns on his resume? In actuality, there are no milestones or benchmarks that guarantee membership in the national pastime's most exclusive fraternity.

As it stands today, there are five ways in which to be elected to the National Baseball Hall of Fame. It begins with the Baseball Writers' Association of America holding an annual election for players with at least 10 years of Big League experience who have been retired for at least five years but not more than 20. The majority of inductees reach Cooperstown by way of the BBWAA. There are also committees to consider managers, umpires, executives and long-retired players, grouped by era, with elections held annually based on time period. Big Leaguers who played prior to US involvement in World War II (1943) are voted on every five years.

Electors vote from a list prepared by the Screening Committee, consisting of six baseball writers appointed by the BBWAA. The ballots are distributed around Thanksgiving and voters have until Dec. 31 to return ballots, with results announced in early January.

Although the specific methods of each committee may vary, there are over-arching commonalities among the four distinct bodies when it comes to voting on candidates. The main regulation, of course, is that players need to receive votes on at least 75 percent of the ballots cast to be elected.

While the rules for election do state that voting should consider the individual's on-field record, overall skill and ability, they also mandate that electors look at a player's value to the game with a wider lens. The rules mention a player's integrity, his sportsmanship and character, and his contribution to the game of baseball as well as to the teams on which he played. Although otherworldly statistics don't hurt, there are no automatic elections based on performances such as hitting the elusive .400 mark in a season, pitching a perfect game or similar outstanding achievements.

Regardless of his resume, any person designated as ineligible by the Office of the Commissioner of Major League Baseball will not appear on the ballot unless that status changes. And in all cases, the Hall of Fame's Board of Directors reserves the right to revoke, alter or amend the rules at any time.

Veterans Committee

OF THE 292 INDIVIDUALS THAT HAVE HAD THE HONOR OF BEING inducted into the Baseball Hall of Fame entering 2010, 157 (94 Major League players, 26 executives, 19 managers, nine Negro Leaguers and nine umpires) were inducted thanks to the Baseball Hall of Fame Committee on Veterans, more commonly referred to as the Veterans Committee throughout its several incarnations.

In August 1935, with the official dedication of the Cooperstown shrine already scheduled for 1939, officials at the Hall of Fame and from Major League Baseball were under pressure to determine a process by which to elect Hall of Famers to the fledgling shrine. It was announced that 10 players — five from the 1800s and five from the 1900s — would be voted on by the BBWAA to form the Hall's first class. Later that year the numbers were revised to 10 modern players and five players from before 1900.

In the first vote, 78 retired players, officials and baseball writers cast ballots for a total of 58 players from the 19th century. None received the required 75 percent.

With subsequent votes also failing to elect any players from baseball's early decades, it wasn't until the annual baseball meetings in Chicago in December 1937 that it was announced that the Centennial Committee, consisting of Commissioner Kenesaw Mountain Landis, American League President Will Harridge and National League President Ford Frick, had selected five "Builders of Baseball" for the Hall of Fame: George Wright, Morgan Bulkeley, Ban Johnson, John McGraw and Connie Mack. They were chosen, it was explained, not only for their playing ability, but also "for their inspiration to baseball in its early years." The Centennial Committee added Henry Chadwick and Alexander Cartwright in 1938.

With an outcry that the great players from the 1800s were being ignored, it was announced in May 1939, just a month before the Hall of Fame's inaugural induction ceremony, that Landis, Harridge and Frick had selected A.G. Spalding, Charles Radbourn, Cap Anson, Candy Cummings, Buck Ewing and Charles Comiskey as the newest members of the Hall of Fame.

An "Old-Timers Committee" was appointed by Landis in August 1944 to look closely at players who were active prior to 1910 for possible enshrinement in Cooperstown. Less than a month after Landis's death on Nov. 25, 1944, this newly formed committee voted unanimously to make the longtime commissioner a bona fide Hall of Famer.

Despite good intentions, both the Centennial Committee and the Old-Timers Committee failed to formalize their election processes. In an effort to correct this oversight and formalize the election rules, an 11-member Baseball Hall of Fame Committee on Veterans, made up of baseball executives and the press, was established in 1953. This new committee would hold elections every two years, with eligible players having been retired for at least 25 years and managers and umpires for at least five years.

Controversially, the Veterans Committee would be considering players that had once been passed over by the BBWAA. That didn't sit well with some of the writers. "Most members of the Veterans Committee have been in adversarial positions with regard to the writers virtually all their baseball lives," wrote longtime hardball scribe Harold Rosenthal. "They're not going to pay much attention now."

For the next five decades the Veterans Committee operated under the same basic rules, electing more than 100 candidates to the Hall of Fame (22 in the 1960s, 32 in the 1970s, 17 in the 1980s and 25 in the 1990s). Some of the greatest names from baseball's long history were included during these years — baseball legends representing all scopes of the game from Al Lopez to Miller Huggins, Branch Rickey to Jocko Conlan, Casey Stengel to Phil Rizzuto.

In 2001, the Hall of Fame's board of directors made the process more accessible, while maintaining the high standards for earning election, with a restructuring of the process. The revised Veterans Committee procedures included replacing the 15-member Veterans Committee with a group comprised of the living members of the Baseball Hall of Fame and the living recipients of the J.G. Taylor Spink and Ford C. Frick awards. These Hall of Famers were supplemented by longstanding Veterans Committee members whose terms had not yet expired.

With no electees to emerge for three voting cycles, the board made alterations to the committee again in 2007. In addition to the separate pre-1943 player voting every five years, there are currently three ballots voted on every other year — players, managers/umpires and executives/pioneers — reviewed by three small electorates made up of players, executives and writers.

Altered in July 2010, voting committees now consider three eras in baseball's history: Expansion (1973–89), Golden (1947–72) and Pre-Integration (1871–1946). The committees will convene on an annual rotating basis, starting at the winter meetings with the Expansion Era, to consider managers, umpires, executives and long-retired players for election. Of course, any eligible candidate to earn 75 percent of the vote through these committees will be enshrined the following summer in Cooperstown.

Dodgers Owner Walter O'Malley (left), who was elected by the Veterans Committee in 2008, and Manager Walter Alston.

Hall Call

THE LUCKY TASK OF INFORMING FORMER BIG LEAGUE BASEBALL players that they've reached the game's greatest height has been the joyful responsibility of two men over the past four decades — the late Jack Lang and Jack O'Connell — along with Hall of Fame Chairman Jane Forbes Clark, who is first to congratulate the new members.

As secretary-treasurer of the Baseball Writers' Association of America, both conducted the voting for the organization's annual awards: Most Valuable Player, Cy Young Award, Rookie of the Year and Manager of the Year. Another part of the job includes helping to tally the BBWAA votes for election to the National Baseball Hall of Fame and calling those who have received at least 75 percent of the votes cast and giving them the good news.

O'Connell, once a writer with the New York *Daily News* and *Hartford Courant*, has been making these life-changing phone calls since 1995.

"I'm doing something millions of people would love to do," says O'Connell. "I tell them, and it's not just a line, 'This is just the beginning to a whole new life.'"

Dubbed "the voice of heaven" by former knuckleballer Phil Niekro (who was elected in 1997), O'Connell has encountered the full spectrum of emotions on the other end of the line.

"I remember George Brett and Don Sutton bawling like babies. It's so emotional," says O'Connell. "Actually, Brett didn't start crying until I told him that he was going in with Nolan Ryan and Robin Yount. When he heard that Robin was going in with him, it wasn't just crying. It was uncontrollable crying."

Informing Eddie Murray in 2003 may have been the most trying call of O'Connell's tenure, as the longtime first baseman was in a limousine heading to his sister's funeral when O'Connell finally got through. O'Connell, who had only been made aware of the funeral plans the previous day, first got no answer when he called Murray's cell phone but he eventually got through on Murray's wife's cell phone. She told O'Connell that her husband could not take any calls.

"I didn't think she was making the connection, so I said, 'Believe me, Mrs. Murray, he wants to take this call. It will take five seconds.' I could hear Eddie in the background say, 'I'll take this call,'" O'Connell recalls. "All he said was, 'Thank you. Thank you very much.' And then he got quiet."

Also in 2003, O'Connell reached catcher Gary "Kid" Carter on a golf course and got a different reaction.

"'Kid, it's Jack O'Connell.' I didn't say another word. The next thing I hear is screaming. 'Yes, I'm in! I'm in! I'm in!'" says O'Connell. "He finally got back on the phone and said, 'This is great news.' I told him, 'What? I haven't told you anything yet.' I felt like joking and saying, 'I was just seeing whether you had Eddie Murray's number.' But I didn't have the heart."

O'Connell says that players have different ways of dealing with the anticipation of getting the call.

"I remember when Dennis Eckersley made it [in 2004]. He was a nervous wreck. He told me that he didn't sleep for two days. He couldn't eat," says O'Connell. "And he asked me, 'How does [Bruce] Sutter do it, keep waiting year after year?'"

Former relief pitcher Sutter waited by the telephone every January for more than a decade before finally getting that all-important call in 2006.

"I told Sutter, 'It took 13 years, but I think we finally got it right.' He's a Hall of Famer now. This is just the beginning. He's stepping into immortality. He's in Cooperstown. His life will never be the same."

Holding the responsibility prior to O'Connell was Lang, who, from 1967 to 1994, called to give the news to legends including Willie Mays, Hank Aaron, Mickey Mantle and Tom Seaver. He let 44 Hall of Famers know that they had reached the pinnacle of the national pastime. Lang, who spent the majority of his career with the *Long Island Press* and the New York *Daily News*, was nicknamed the "good news man" by former Chicago Cubs outfielder and 1987 Hall of Fame inductee Billy Williams.

"I got to call the winners. You have no idea what a joy that is," Lang once said. "I use the same phrase for everybody. I just say, 'Congratulations, you've just been elected to the Baseball Hall of Fame.'"

While Lang would only call the electees, he made an exception with Roy Campanella, the former Brooklyn Dodgers catcher who was paralyzed as the result of a 1958 car accident.

"Campy told me that in his situation he would need advance notice to get to New York for a press conference if he made the Hall. He was the only person I called when he didn't make it," Lang said. "They were tough calls because he didn't get in until his fifth year on the ballot [1969]. That was a very satisfying call."

Lang says that the most memorable call he made went to Joe Medwick in 1968. As a 13-year-old kid in 1934, he had seen Medwick in a barnstorming game on Long Island and gotten his autograph.

"Thirty-five years later I called to tell him that he was in the Hall of Fame," Lang said. "It was quite an honor."

Lang passed away in 2007, but not before getting a special call informing him that he would be honored with the J.G. Taylor Spink Award for "meritorious service to baseball writing" at the 1986 Hall of Fame Induction Ceremony, alongside players Bobby Doerr, Ernie Lombardi and Willie McCovey.

Following spread, from left: Orlando Cepeda, Robin Yount, Nolan Ryan and George Brett accept their plaques during the 1999 Induction Ceremony.

On April 18, 1981, Reds ace Tom Seaver struggled through one of his worst innings of the season. An error, a walk, a double, a sacrifice fly and a single allowed St. Louis to score three runs in the fourth frame. But with a runner on base and two outs, Seaver showed why they called him "Tom Terrific," striking out Keith Hernandez to end the threat. It was the 3,000th punchout of Seaver's illustrious career, making him the fifth pitcher in history to join that lofty club.

Strikeouts had always been a key component of Seaver's game. When the fresh-faced Southern Cal alum burst onto the New York scene in 1967, he was named Rookie of the Year after whiffing 170 batters, the eighth-highest total of all time for a first-year pitcher. Two years later, he led the Mets to one of history's unlikeliest world championships — a title that was keyed by a dramatic strikeout of Baltimore's Paul Blair in Game 4 of the World Series. With the game tied, 1-1, and the winning run on third for the Orioles in the 10th, Seaver whiffed Blair to end the inning, and in the bottom of the frame his Mets teammates were able to score the winning run.

Four starts later — in his fourth outing of the 1970 season — Seaver etched his name in the record books by tying the record for most strikeouts in a nine-inning game, with 19. Seaver tied the record against the San Diego Padres in style, striking out the last 10 consecutive batters he faced. He would win five NL strikeout titles in the 1970s, and his career total of 3,640 ranked third on the all-time list at the time of his retirement after the 1986 season. Seaver's glove and the ball from his 3,000th strikeout, pictured above, are two of the Hall's most treasured artifacts.

ORLANDO MANUEL CEPEDA PENNES
"BABY BULL" "CHA-CHA"
SAN FRANCISCO, N.L. 1958 – 1966; ST. LOUIS, N.L. 1966 – 1968
ATLANTA, N.L. 1969 – 1972; OAKLAND, A.L. 1972
BOSTON, A.L. 1973; KANSAS CITY, A.L. 1974

A POWERFUL FIRST BASEMAN AND CONSISTENT RUN PRODUCER FOR
17 MAJOR LEAGUE SEASONS, NOTWITHSTANDING CHRONIC KNEE
PROBLEMS. HIS ABILITY TO DRIVE THE BALL WITH AUTHORITY
WAS RESPECTED AND FEARED BY THE OPPOSITION UNANIMOUS
SELECTION FOR BOTH THE 1958 N.L. ROOKIE OF THE YEAR AWARD
AND 1967 MVP HONORS. THE 11-TIME ALL STAR LED THE N.L. IN
HOME RUNS (46) AND RBI (142) IN 1961 BATTED .300 NINE TIMES AND
SLUGGED 379 HOME RUNS. HIS STALWART LEADERSHIP PROPELLED
HIS CLUBS TO THREE WORLD SERIES

ROBIN R. YOUNT
MILWAUKEE, A.L. 1974 – 1993

A PROLIFIC HITTER WITH A STRONG DEMEANOR WHO WAS
EQUALLY GRACEFUL AT SHORTSTOP AND IN CENTER FIELD. ONE
OF THREE PLAYERS TO EARN MVP HONORS AT TWO POSITIONS.
PRODUCED 3,142 HITS, 7TH MOST IN AMERICAN LEAGUE HISTORY
HIT .300 SIX TIMES, 40 DOUBLES FOUR TIMES, 10 OR MORE
TRIPLES AND SCORED 100 RUNS FIVE TIMES. EXCEPTIONAL
CONDITIONING AND EXTRAORDINARY WORK ETHIC MADE HIM A
PARAGON OF CONSISTENCY AND DURABILITY FOR 20 SEASONS.
BECAME AN EVERY DAY MAJOR LEAGUER AT AGE 18.

"I WOULD LIKE TO SAY MY FAVORITE HERO WAS MUHAMMAD ALI. HE SAID AT ONE TIME, 'I AM THE GREATEST.' THAT IS SOMETHING I ALWAYS WANTED TO BE. AND NOW THAT THE ASSOCIATION HAS VOTED ME INTO THE BASEBALL HALL OF FAME, MY JOURNEY AS A PLAYER IS COMPLETE. I AM NOW IN THE CLASS OF THE GREATEST PLAYERS OF ALL TIME AND AT THIS MOMENT, I AM … VERY, VERY HUMBLED."

RICKEY HENDERSON, JULY 26, 2009

SANDY KOUFAX

INDUCTED IN 1972

BASEBALL DIE-HARDS have always relished controversy and debate, making what happened during the mid-1960s all the more remarkable. One man gave baseball something that it rarely had: unanimity.

Ballplayers, fans, managers and just about everyone who had ever watched ball meet bat were in agreement that Sandy Koufax was pitching better than anyone had before him. The southpaw from Brooklyn, who had been inked to a contract by his hometown Dodgers in 1954, won the pitching Triple Crown in the National League in 1963, 1965 and 1966 and was the unanimous Cy Young Award winner all three years. He twirled three no-hitters and a perfect game during that dominant stretch, won the NL MVP Award, set the modern single-season strikeout record, set the record for most strikeouts in a World Series game, was named MVP of the 1963 Fall Classic and made believers on both coasts.

"I can see how he won 25 games," Yogi Berra said while reflecting on Koufax's '63 campaign, during which L.A. swept Berra's Yankees in the World Series. "What I don't understand is how he lost five."

While he was at the peak of his powers it seemed like a shock whenever anyone even scratched a hit off of Koufax, let alone handed him a loss. Sadly, arthritis forced his early retirement, but soon after, Koufax became the youngest player ever enshrined in the Hall of Fame at age 36.

Ted Williams' Message

It was partly cloudy and 86 degrees outside, a typical mid-summer day in the small village of Cooperstown, N.Y., but the lithe hitting machine known as the "Splendid Splinter" was about to shake things up. His remarks before a worldwide audience would forever change the course of baseball's most cherished institution.

Ted Williams, the former Boston Red Sox slugger, arguably the greatest hitter in the game's long history, was to be inducted into the National Baseball Hall of Fame on July 25, 1966. Sharing the stage with him this day was beloved Manager Casey Stengel, an electee after 54 years in professional baseball, well known for his unique gift of gab. But it would be a day for Teddy Ballgame to make news with his words instead of his bat.

What began as a standard acceptance speech evolved into something more, when at the end Williams spoke for those without a voice, those who had been shunted aside, those with no hope of ever joining the national pastime's fabled fraternity: "Inside this building are plaques dedicated to baseball men of all generations and I'm privileged to join them … And I hope that someday the names of Satchel Paige and Josh Gibson in some way can be added as a symbol of the great Negro players that are not here only because they were not given a chance."

Why Williams decided to use this day to make his case is up for debate. But the groundbreaking statement by one of baseball's greats, though previously made by others in less prestigious forums, would prove to be the impetus for change.

"His speech had an impact. He did change some minds," said Hall of Famer and Negro Leagues veteran Monte Irvin, as quoted in the book *Ted Williams: A Tribute*. "The writers picked up on it, and some of the powers-that-be at the Hall of Fame had to kind of perk up and take notice."

The *Washington Post* sportswriter and 1975 J.G. Taylor Spink Award recipient Shirley Povich was more succinct, later penning: "The fact is that Ted Williams launched the whole movement for the inclusion of Negro Leagues players into the Hall of Fame at Cooperstown."

It became reality on Feb. 3, 1971, when Commissioner Bowie Kuhn announced the formation of a special 10-man panel, the Committee on Negro League Veterans, which included Roy Campanella, Judy Johnson and Monte Irvin, to select the top Negro Leagues stars of the pre-1947 era "as part of a new exhibit commemorating the contributions of the Negro Leagues to baseball." But they weren't to be official members of the Hall, as they hadn't played in the Major Leagues for the required 10 seasons.

Allowed to choose one player per year, the Committee unanimously selected Paige on Feb. 9, 1971. The tall and lean right-handed pitcher, whose true age was forever up for debate, filled stadiums wherever he pitched with fans eager to see one of baseball's greatest hurlers. "I don't feel segregated," said Paige at a press conference that day. "I'm proud to be wherever they put me in the Hall of Fame." Not all agreed.

"If the blacks go in as a special thing, it's not worth a hill of beans. It's the same rotten thing all over again," said Hall of Famer Jackie Robinson, who broke down Big League baseball's color barrier in 1947. "They deserve to be in it but not as black players in a special category. Rules have been changed before. You can change rules like you change laws if the law is unjust."

The rules were changed on July 8, 1971, with Kuhn and Hall of Fame President Paul Kerr announcing that Paige and future inductees would be given full membership. So it was on Aug. 9, 1971, five years and two weeks after Williams made his bold pronouncement, that Paige did indeed became a bona fide Hall of Famer. "I am the proudest man on the earth today," he said.

Hall of Fame Weekend

Hall of Fame Weekend is the highlight of Cooperstown's civic calendar. Planning the event is a year-round job for many staff members, and starts again almost immediately after a the current edition ends.

"From the moment an Induction Weekend ends, we are evaluating, reviewing and preparing for the next induction class and ceremony," says Whitney Selover, the Hall of Fame's director of special events and travel. "The weekend requires the participation and focus of the entire Hall of Fame staff, along with others brought on board for the weekend and a full team of volunteers, to serve in capacities ranging from hospitality

for returning Hall of Famers and new inductees, security, media relations, visitor services, transportation and so much more.

"Our goal is that everything during Hall of Fame Weekend runs like clockwork, so that we can be available to meet the needs of our very special guests, from Hall of Fame members to our Museum visitors, 24 hours a day and to make the weekend as enjoyable and memorable for them as they could possibly imagine."

Held annually over the weekend of the last Sunday of July, the four-day celebration of baseball history is full of family activities and

Ted Williams (left) and then-MLB Commissioner William Eckert during the 1966 Induction Ceremony.

is highlighted by the Induction Ceremony on Sunday afternoon. It's here that the game's immortals are recognized and forever enshrined in the Hall of Fame's Plaque Gallery. Weather permitting, the ceremony takes place on the grounds of the Clark Sports Center, located on lower Susquehanna Avenue, just one mile south of the Hall of Fame.

In recent years, the weekend's action has started with Hall of Fame shortstop Ozzie Smith headlining a fundraiser for the Museum's education programs at Doubleday Field on Friday. At the event, participants get the chance to interact with Smith and a few of his fellow Hall of Famers on the ballfield for two hours.

Saturday's schedule typically involves such events as Connecting Generations, a popular program held at the Clark Sports Center that allows visitors to compete in a trivia contest with baseball icons; an annual New York–Penn League game at the legendary Doubleday Field; and the Hall of Fame Legends Parade, where the returning Hall of Famers ride down Main Street on their way to a private reception at the Hall of Fame.

The newest members of the Hall assist in bringing the busy weekend to an end when they participate in a Legends Series question-and-answer event at the Clark Sports Center on Monday morning.

Hall of Fame President

FROM HIS GIG SELLING HOT DOGS AT BOSTON'S FENWAY PARK IN high school to his current role as president of the National Baseball Hall of Fame, Jeff Idelson has spent most of his life turning his passion for baseball into his livelihood. His hard work and determination have led him from the cramped concourses of one of the game's green cathedrals to the hallowed corridors in Cooperstown.

The West Newton, Mass., native and 1986 graduate of Connecticut College in New London, Conn., held a number of positions with the Red Sox in the late 1980s, including an internship and subsequent job with the team's public relations department and a producer position for the Red Sox Radio Network. Switching provincial allegiances, he served as director of media relations and publicity for the New York Yankees from 1989–93, after being hired initially as the club's assistant director of media relations. Idelson worked as assistant vice president and press officer for World Cup USA in 1994, when the international event enjoyed its highest-ever attendance. Idelson then joined the Baseball Hall of Fame as director of public relations and promotions. He was promoted to vice president of communications and education in 1999, and was named to his current title in 2008.

"It's a multi-faceted position," Idelson reflects. "It's overseeing our full-time staff of 100 and our part-time staff of another 100 in the summer. It's assuring that the Hall of Fame is continuing to be made as accessible as possible to as wide an audience as possible. It's maintaining the high standards set before me by the others who have held this position. It's working with our living Hall of Famers and our 17 board members. It involves a little bit of everything."

Idelson and his staff are always looking for innovative ways to share the history of America's pastime with fans around the globe, including utilizing new technologies and social media.

"It's preserving and protecting the game's history and telling it to as wide an audience as possible, and making our collections, our lifeblood,

as accessible as possible to as wide an audience as possible. That's our mission: making it accessible and preserving the game's history."

Having overseen the daily affairs of the Hall since taking over as president in 2008, it should come as no surprise that while Induction Day is hectic, he finds it a highlight of his year.

"It's not only the greatest celebration of Hall of Famers in one place at any time," Idelson explains. "I also find great pride in seeing the smiles on the faces of tens of thousands of fans who come to witness baseball's greatest individual achievement, which is enshrinement into the Hall of Fame."

Idelson's Induction day begins at 6 a.m. with a check of the weather forecast. An hour later, he's at the office finalizing his opening remarks for the ceremony. By 8 it's on to Leatherstocking Golf Course to visit with the legends participating in the Hall of Famer Golf Tournament.

Whatever remains of Idelson's jam-packed morning is spent at the Otesaga Resort Hotel, first meeting with Hall of Fame staff on any unresolved issues, then breakfast with special guests, and finally, after a quick trip home to change clothes, Idelson hops on a bus headed to the Induction Ceremony.

Arriving at the Clark Sports Center property at around 12:30 p.m., Idelson meets with his staff and helps to line up Hall of Famers on stage in order of introduction.

Idelson can be found on the Induction Ceremony stage from 1 to 4 p.m., delivering his opening remarks at approximately 1:30. Afterward, at around 4:30, he boards a bus back to the Otesaga for photos, a cocktail party and dinner with the Hall of Famers.

After dinner ends at 9 p.m., it's off to the Otesaga's Templeton Lounge, where Idelson can be found visiting with newly minted Hall of Famers and guests. His night officially comes to an end when he heads home at 2 a.m. to try and get some sleep … because the next day is another busy one.

Voice of Induction Day

VETERAN BASEBALL ANNOUNCER GEORGE GRANDE KNOWS A GOOD thing when he sees it.

Grande, who has called games for ESPN, the New York Yankees, the St. Louis Cardinals and, most recently, the Cincinnati Reds, has served as the voice of the National Baseball Hall of Fame Induction Ceremony — introducing the returning Hall of Fame members — since 1981. Grande was working for ESPN when the idea of having a regular voice of Induction Day first came up.

"At that time they would just basically say, 'Ladies and gentlemen, here are our returning Hall of Famers,' and everybody would walk out on the podium and they'd give one long round of applause for the whole group. Bill Guilfoile [former Hall Vice President] had the idea that we should really do something more, something that would be certainly the right way to treat what is the royalty of the game of baseball," Grande explains. "So we talked a little bit about it and Bill said, 'What do you think?' I said, 'It sure makes a lot of sense. What you should do is get somebody like an Ernie Harwell, Mel Allen or a Jack Buck to come in and do it.'"

Unlike the broadcasting luminaries he suggested, Grande was not bound to one Big League club, making him an ideal fit. He was eventually asked to assume the role.

"It's just an honor for me," Grande says, "as it would be for anybody that loves the game and anybody that's ever been a part of the game. I look at myself as a fan that has the great honor of stepping up there and welcoming the people that we've all enjoyed and adored over the years."

Grande, a 42-year veteran of the broadcasting business and the voice of Reds TV from 1993 until he stepped down after the 2009 season, has become ingrained in the game. The New Haven, Conn., native was good enough to play for the University of Southern California in the late 1960s with such future Big League players as Tom Seaver, Bill Lee and Brent Strom. He was also a utility infielder on Southern Cal's 1968 national championship team.

Over the years, no employer turned down Grande's request to return to Cooperstown for the ceremony during the middle of the summer. "Wherever I've worked, the one thing that I ask is if the Hall of Fame asks, that you allow me to go to the ceremonies," he says. "And everybody has said 'Sure.'"

As for the actual introductions of the Hall of Famers, Grande says once he knows the order in which they will enter the stage, he tries to figure out what would tie one to another, such as milestone anniversaries of great moments. But he does occasionally get special requests.

"Some of the men who went into the service asked me not to talk about baseball but to talk about their service," Grande says. "Enos Slaughter said, 'Please, whatever you do don't talk about the Mad Dash. That's all anybody mentions. They never say I was a .300 hitter.'"

And Grande, who missed the 2005 Hall of Fame induction due to family illnesses, says he has cherished every bit of the very unique responsibility that he has had for the Hall.

"I'm happy for what I've had and I enjoy every step of the way," he says. "As long as they keep asking, I'll keep coming."

Media Presence

DIE-HARD BASEBALL FANS THAT CAN'T MAKE IT TO COOPERSTOWN for the Hall of Fame Induction Ceremony don't have to feel like they're missing out on all the fun, thanks to the strong media attention that the annual event attracts.

The National Baseball Hall of Fame's public relations department estimates that it credentials between 400 and 500 media for the weekend of activities each July, with an all-time high of approximately 900 registered members of the media on hand for the enshrinement of Cal Ripken Jr. and Tony Gwynn in 2007.

"All eyes of the baseball world are upon us," says Brad Horn, senior director of communications and education. "What that has meant is that the biggest names in baseball media have converged on Cooperstown, and it's the one opportunity for us as a Hall of Fame to present ourselves in the best and brightest light."

Along with Communications Director Craig Muder, Horn and his staff provide first-class service to media from around the globe, a contingent estimated at 45 percent print and online outlets (including national baseball writers from *The New York Times*, *Chicago Tribune*, *Los Angeles Times*, *USA Today*, MLB.com, Yahoo!, ESPN.com and The Associated Press), 25 percent television reporters (including MLB Network and ESPN) and 30 percent radio broadcasters (including Sirius XM).

"Induction Weekend is the best thing I cover," says *Houston Chronicle* sports columnist Richard Justice. "An hour inside the Hall of Fame will melt the stress away and remind you why you loved baseball in the first place. It's absolutely magical. And then sitting there Sunday afternoon and seeing Frank Robinson and Bob Gibson and Hank Aaron and the others take their places, it's a trip back through the years and so many special times."

J.G. Taylor Spink Award

THE J.G. TAYLOR SPINK AWARD, NAMED AFTER THE PIONEERING publisher of *The Sporting News*, has been voted upon annually since 1962. It honors one baseball writer each year and is presented at the Hall of Fame Induction Ceremony by that year's president of the Baseball Writers' Association of America.

The BBWAA honored Spink by naming the award after him, and presenting it to writers for their "meritorious service to the national sport and to our profession." Spink died on Dec. 7, 1962, just two months after the BBWAA sanctioned the award, but his name lives on through the greatest honor that a baseball journalist can achieve, as an honoree of the Hall of Fame.

Acclaimed writers honored over the years include Ring Lardner (1963), Grantland Rice (1966), Damon Runyon (1967), Fried Lieb (1972), Shirley Povich (1975), Red Smith (1976), Dick Young (1978), Jim Murray (1987), Jerome Holtzman (1989), Leonard Koppett (1992),

Wendell Smith (1993), Sam Lacy (1997), Murray Chass (2003) and Peter Gammons (2004).

Spink Award voting has undergone numerous changes over the years. Today, a Spink Award committee studies nominations from various regional chapters and decides on three writers during a conference call prior to the All-Star Game, where the ballot is announced.

Ballots are mailed to BBWAA members with 10 or more consecutive years of service each November with the winner (based on a simple majority vote, as opposed to the 75 percent needed in the players' elections) announced at the winter meetings. Since 2002, it has been determined by a mail ballot, similar to the BBWAA's Hall of Fame election, among more than 500 Hall of Fame voting members of the BBWAA.

A Spink Award recipient is presented with a certificate during the Induction Ceremony and recognized in the *Scribes & Mikemen* exhibit in the Museum Library.

Ford C. Frick Award

THEY'RE THE VOICES OF SUMMER, WORDSMITHS WHO MADE THE game of baseball come alive on radio and television, and the best of the best are honored in Cooperstown.

The Ford C. Frick Award has been presented annually by the Hall of Fame and Museum since 1978 to a broadcaster for "major contributions to baseball." It's named for the 1970 Hall of Fame enshrinee who first made a name for himself as a radio broadcaster in the 1930s before serving as Commissioner of Baseball from 1951–65.

When the announcement of the establishment of the award was made on June 21, 1978, by then–Hall of Fame President Ed Stack, he said, "Broadcasters are an important part of the national game, and we want to recognize those who excel."

The Hall of Fame did just that, recognizing illustrious voices such as Mel Allen, Ernie Harwell, Vin Scully and Lindsey Nelson. The Frick Award isn't limited to English-speaking broadcasters, as Spanish-language

announcers including Buck Canel (1985), Jaime Jarrin (1998) and Felo Ramirez (2001) also have been honored.

Ten finalists for the Frick Award are selected each January, including three fan selections from an online vote conducted by the Hall of Fame. The seven other finalists are chosen by a Hall of Fame research committee. The electorate is comprised of the living Frick Award recipients and five broadcast historians/columnists.

Frick Award voters are asked to base their selections on the following criteria: longevity; continuity with a club; honors, including national assignments such as the World Series and All-Star Games; and popularity with fans.

To be considered, an active or retired broadcaster must have at least 10 years of continuous Major League broadcast service with a ballclub, a network or a combination of the two. Typically, more than 200 broadcasters are eligible for consideration in any one year.

With the Cardinals having mauled the Tigers, 8-3, in the opener of the 1934 World Series, Game 2 took on added significance for the 43,451 fans who showed up at Detroit's Navin Field. It was the Motor City's first World Series appearance in a quarter century — since 1909, when Ty Cobb was 22 — and fans were salivating at the possibility of the first world title in team history.

They had good reason to be optimistic, for the Tigers had won 101 regular-season games that year to set a new franchise record. The backbone of Detroit's team was its remarkable infield — first baseman Hank Greenberg, second baseman Charlie Gehringer, third baseman Marv Owen and shortstop Billy Rogell — who combined to drive in 462 runs while each batted at least .296. The 23-year-old Greenberg, playing his first full Major League season, batted .339, while the veteran Gehringer hit at a .356 clip.

The Tigers entered the bottom of the ninth in Game 2 trailing, 2-1, but there was a spark of hope when Pete Fox opened the inning with a single. Starting hurler Schoolboy Rowe, a .303 hitter, was allowed to bat for himself and laid down a sacrifice bunt. Gee Walker followed with a foul pop-up between home and first, but the Cardinals, in a defensive miscommunication, allowed it to drop untouched. Given a reprieve, Walker singled to send the game into extra innings. Rowe proceeded to make Detroit skipper Mickey Cochrane look brilliant for leaving him in the game, as the young righty mowed down the Cards in the 10th, 11th and 12th while allowing just one baserunner. Finally, in the bottom of the 12th, veteran Goose Goslin lined a single to center for the game-winning run. Despite the dramatic victory, though, the Tigers would end up dropping the Series in seven games. Fans can revisit the legendary game in the Hall, where a ticket from the contest, shown below, is on display.

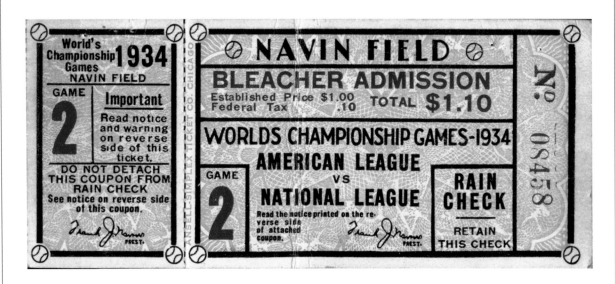

TONY GWYNN

INDUCTED IN 2007

As a young athlete, Tony Gwynn was recruited by San Diego State's basketball team as a point guard, He still holds the school's single-season and career assist records. His dual-threat skills were on display during the weekend of March 7–9, 1981, when Gwynn had a 16-point, 16-assist game in basketball, followed by a baseball doubleheader in which he drove in the winning run in both games. Three months later, Major League Baseball's San Diego Padres and the NBA's Los Angeles Clippers drafted him on the same day.

In 1984, Gwynn won his first batting title. By 1987, he had become a stellar all-around player, batting a league-best .370 while also stealing 56 bases and snaring one of his five Gold Gloves. From 1993 through 1997 he batted at least .350 each year, winning four of his NL-record eight batting titles. The quintessential hitting guru, it was Gwynn who popularized the use of video to study and perfect his mechanics.

Gwynn's finest moment came in 1994, when he snuck achingly close to the .400 mark. His average hovered in the .380s most of the year, but in early August it surged. When a players' strike ended the season on Aug. 12, Gwynn's average stood at .394, the highest since Ted Williams' .406, accomplished 53 years earlier. "My father said if you work hard, good things will happen," Gwynn said in his Hall of Fame induction speech. "Boy, oh boy, he was absolutely right."

"WHEN YOU LOVE A GAME LIKE THIS, YOU'RE NOT WORRYING ABOUT YOUR PAYCHECKS ON THE 1ST AND 15TH. WHEN YOU'RE PLAYING, MONEY IS NO OBJECT. I KNOW, I PLAYED NINE YEARS FOR NOTHING. BUT GOD KNOWS IT WAS THE SILVER LINING AT THE END, TOO. BUT I LOVED IT AS MUCH IN THE MAJOR LEAGUES AS I DID THE FIRST NINE THAT I PLAYED FOR PRACTICALLY NOTHING. IT'S OUR NATIONAL PASTIME, REGARDLESS OF WHAT SIDE OF THE FENCE IT MAY BE."

ROY CAMPANELLA, JULY 28, 1969

INDUCTION
SPEECH

Chapter 3
Treasures

Connie Mack's Philadelphia Athletics undoubtedly expected the 1914 World Series to be more a coronation than a competition. After all, they had breezed to the world title in two of the previous three seasons, and in the 1914 Series they faced what appeared to be their weakest opponent yet — Boston's "Miracle Braves."

The Braves hadn't posted a winning season in 11 years, a stretch that was loaded with embarrassing records like 44-107 and 45-108. On July 20, 1914, they were in last place again, albeit with a not-terrible record of 36-43. From that point forward, though, it seemed as if they couldn't lose. Boston put together a six-game winning streak, and followed it almost immediately with a nine-game streak, and then a seven-gamer. By Aug. 25 — barely a month after being in last — they were tied for first place. The Braves coasted down the home stretch, easily winning the NL pennant.

That was where everyone thought the miracle would end, as fans and pundits alike expected Boston to be obliterated in the World Series by the mighty A's. The Philadelphia lineup, after all, featured the famed "$100,000 Infield" with future Hall of Famers Eddie Collins at second base and Home Run Baker at third. The A's pitching staff also featured seven hurlers with double-digit wins, all of whom had ERAs of 3.06 or better. The A's oozed blue-blooded royalty; the Braves were stray dogs. In the Series, though, the stray dogs grabbed hold of Philadelphia's leg and refused to let go. After a 7-1 blowout win in Game 1, the Braves prevailed in two nail-biters, 1-0 and 5-4. They capped off history's most unlikely sweep with a 3-1 victory over the A's at Fenway Park in Game 4. It was, as one contemporary sportswriter observed, "the most stunning surprise ever dealt the base ball world." Experience one of baseball's biggest upsets at the Hall, where press pins from the 1914 World Series are on display.

Hardball Treasures

In the beginning, there was just an old baseball with its cover ripped wide open.

When the National Baseball Hall of Fame and Museum collected its first artifact — the famed Doubleday Baseball — its mission was to "establish, equip, maintain and operate a repository to collect, classify, preserve and protect records, relics, articles and other items of historic significance connected with or pertaining to the origin, development and growth of baseball."

Today, the institution's collections contain more than 38,000 three-dimensional artifacts representing every facet of the game, from the middle of the 19th century to the present day. The three-dimensional artifacts in the Museum include bats, balls, uniforms, player equipment, ballpark artifacts, awards, artwork, textiles, tickets and assorted memorabilia.

"These collections are the foundation of the institution because this material is relied upon to support the public programming, loan program, traveling exhibitions, education programs and research needs," says Director of Collections Sue MacKay, a Cooperstown native who oversees the organization, maintenance and preservation of the Museum's artifacts. "As stewards of the collection, it is our charge to protect the objects for the public for future generations to enjoy."

The items in the Museum's collection — both those on exhibit for visitors to experience and those held in storage — feature more than 500 gloves, 1,900 bats, 900 uniforms, 700 caps, 70 batting helmets, 6,600 balls, 60 catcher's masks and 50 other pieces of catcher's equipment, including chest protectors and shin guards. Impressive as those figures are, the collection has grown slowly. In fact, the Museum received just 16 artifacts in 1938. But it wasn't long before word got out about this new repository for keepsakes from the emerging national pastime, and new items quickly began making their way to Cooperstown at a steady pace.

With the bequests numerous and baseball collectors generous, the Museum set a one-year record in 1963 when it added nearly 4,000 objects to the permanent collection. According to MacKay, the Museum presently acquires between 300 and 400 items per year as donations to the collection.

"Almost daily, we receive calls, e-mails or visits from folks with interesting stories and remarkable artifacts," she says. "For me, it is intriguing to learn not just about the history of the pieces, but also the lives of the donors and their families."

MacKay has worked at the Hall of Fame since 1994, when she was hired as associate registrar. Since then, her job has evolved. As the overseer of collections, MacKay has had an opportunity in her career that very few could ever dream of: an intimate access to every artifact in the Hall of Fame's possession, which includes items from some of the greatest and most historic moments in the national pastime's history. MacKay's current duties have given her a virtually encyclopedic knowledge of baseball ephemera.

Among her favorite items in the collection is the Eckford Baseball Case — a four-sided Victorian glass-and-wood piece that contains a revolving column of Eckford trophy balls from games that the team won during the 1860s. Another MacKay favorite is the catcher's mask that Fred Thayer patented on Feb. 12, 1878. Thayer's mask was the first of its kind and is just the sort of one-of-a-kind treasure that a baseball enthusiast must travel to Cooperstown to see.

Like Thayer's mask, the Hall Cup — the earliest existing World Championship Series trophy, from 1888 when the New York Giants defeated the St. Louis Browns — is another priceless relic from baseball's early days.

A longer list of artifacts that MacKay adores includes the Babe Ruth bat speckled with 28 notches — each one of them representing a home run that it hit — from the 1927 season; a uniform for the Philadelphia Bobbies, a women's baseball team, worn by Edith Houghton in 1922; a handmade bat used by American internees in Germany during World War II; the first catcher's mitt, which is known as the Gunson Mitt and was invented by Joseph B. Gunson of the Kansas City Blues in 1888; and a baseball pulled from the World Trade Center rubble in Manhattan on Sept. 11, 2001.

Unusual Artifacts

Did you know that the National Baseball Hall of Fame and Museum has in its collection a rubber tire that was used by Sandy Koufax to ice down his left arm after pitching games during the mid-1960s? How about a coffee can of Georgia red clay from the baseball diamond in Demorest, Ga., where Hall of Fame slugger and first baseman Johnny Mize got his start in baseball? Former Curator of Collections Peter Clark, who held the title of the Hall's longest-tenured employee when he retired in 2009 after 40 years of service, included them as some of the Museum's most unusual, interesting and unique three-dimensional artifacts.

Other unusual Hall of Fame artifacts on Clark's list include a razor blade used by Hall of Famer Cy Young when he was 86 years old while staying with William Shelton of Akron, Ohio, on Sept. 9, 1953; glasses worn by American League umpire Frank Umont on April 24, 1956, at Kansas City during a contest between the Athletics and the Detroit Tigers (he was the first Major League umpire to wear corrective lenses); and a red felt Shriner's fez that belonged to Hall of Fame outfielder Ty Cobb, who was made a Noble of Moslem Temple in Detroit on Jan. 26, 1912, and an honorary member of the City of Straits Lodge No. 452 on May 7, 1921.

Also among those items that piqued Clark's interest is a bowling pin that was presented to Hall of Famer Rogers Hornsby at Hornsby Bowlers Night — sponsored by the Greater Cincinnati Bowling Proprietors Association — at Crosley Field in Cincinnati on Aug. 22, 1952; a black trombone case that actor Robert Redford used to cart around his character Roy Hobbs' magical bat "Wonderboy" in the 1984 film *The Natural*; a boomerang presented to former National League President John Heydler in 1938 and autographed by the players who participated in that year's Victorian Baseball Council (representing West Australia, South Australia, Victoria and New South Wales); one half of home plate from the New York Mets' former home field Shea Stadium — taken from the field after the 1969 World Series in which the Amazin' Mets overtook the Baltimore Orioles 4 games to 1 — donated by two Mets fans from Brooklyn. The whereabouts of the other half is unknown.

Even odder may be the machete belonging to longtime American League President Ban Johnson, used on hunting trips with Chicago White Sox owner Charles Comiskey.

But the strangest artifact Clark has come across?

"That would be Mickey Mantle's toenails," Clark says with a laugh. "A number of years ago we got a letter from a fellow offering to donate Mickey Mantle's toenail clippings that he had gathered in a hotel room in Miami when the Yankees were at Spring Training. The accessions committee turned them down by a unanimous vote."

The Art of Baseball

WHETHER USING OIL ON CANVAS, ACRYLIC ON FIBERBOARD, OR some other combination of media and base, artists have been drawing inspiration from our national game from the sport's beginning. The Frank and Peggy Steele Gallery, located on the National Baseball Hall of Fame and Museum's first floor, is home to *The Art of Baseball* exhibit, which features representations of the game in fine-art form. The exhibit showcases more than two dozen pieces, spanning in time from "The Little Baseball Player," an 1860 painting by John George Brown with children playing baseball without gloves, to Charles Fazzino's three-dimensional work from 2008 entitled "The Curse is Dead," presenting the frenetic energy of the Red Sox's 2004 World Series title.

"The Hall of Fame's art collection contains a variety of baseball-related fine art, folk art and sculpture," says Hall of Fame Director of Collections Sue MacKay. "The Hall has pieces by Norman Rockwell, Andy Warhol, LeRoy Neiman and cartoons by Charles Schulz and Willard Mullin. The art collection continues to grow as baseball fans transfer their passion for the game to canvas and paper utilizing an assortment of mediums. Baseball and art are a natural combination."

Among the classic works hanging from *The Art of Baseball*'s walls are "Game Called Because of Rain" by Norman Rockwell (oil on canvas, 1949), "Tom Seaver" by Andy Warhol (acrylic screenprint on canvas, 1977), and "The Hall of Famer" by LeRoy Neiman (oil on board, 1996). Sculpture in the exhibit includes "The Base Ball Player" by Jonathan Scott Hartley (bronze, 1886), "Honus Wagner" by William Clark Noble (bronze, 1910), "Chief Bender" by an unknown artist (bronze, 1914), "Christy Mathewson" by Gertrude Boyle Kanno (bronze, 1922), "John Henry 'Pop' Lloyd" by Anthony Frudakis (bronze, 1994), and "Casey Stengel" by Rhoda Sherbell (oil on white gypsum cement, 2004).

Baseball Cards

"I KNEW WHEN MY CAREER WAS OVER," SAID GOOD-HUMORED BIG Leaguer Bob Uecker. "In 1965 my baseball card came out with no picture."

Although the National Baseball Hall of Fame and Museum doesn't have that cardboard keepsake in its collection, the institution's archives contain more than 135,000 baseball cards. A small portion of the Hall of Fame's collection of cardboard treasures is located on the Museum's third floor next to the Education Gallery. And while many fans may consider cards to be mere relics from their youth, the Hall of Fame's collection is

The Eckford Baseball Case. Following spread: The Hall's card collection.

often used for education and research purposes. Those cards that are not on exhibit reside in a climate-controlled storage space.

Along a wall and behind a long glass case sit hundreds of baseball cards, dating from the late 19th century. The cards provide a unique way of charting the evolution of the game. You can see when African-American players first started to appear in the late 1940s, the explosion of Latin American players in the early 1960s, and the bright and colorful card designs from the early 1970s.

Among the most talked about and coveted cards in the collection is the T206 Honus Wagner, a bona fide Holy Grail for collectors because Wagner — a star shortstop for the Pittsburgh Pirates in the early 1900s who was part of the first class of five Hall of Fame electees in 1936 —

halted further production of the card by the American Tobacco Company in 1912 and very few ended up reaching the public. Amongst the Hall of Fame's collection are two of the fabled collectibles. The Hall of Fame acquired its first T206 Wagner when renowned collector Barry Halper donated it in 1984. Edward Stack, the Hall of Fame president at the time that the card was donated, said then that it "adds immeasurably to the Hall of Fame's prestige, and satisfies the curiosity of countless visitors who constantly ask about the card."

The Hall of Fame's second T206 also came from Halper, but this time was purchased by Major League Baseball and donated in 2000. While the Hall of Fame's collection of cards is impressive and spans many eras, it is but a small percentage of those ever produced.

Donations

"KNOWING THAT THERE'S A SMALL PART OF ME, A SMALL PART OF my career on display for people to see forever is something that is pretty cool," said 10-time All-Star pitcher Tom Glavine.

Glavine, who finished his 22-season career with 305 victories, donated the spikes he wore during the 1995 Fall Classic, when his eight frames of one-hit ball in the decisive Game 6 earned him MVP honors with the Braves. He also gave the Hall the Mets jersey that he wore on Aug. 5, 2007, when he recorded his 300th career win. But he's just one of hundreds of players who have been more than happy to donate over the years.

"Building relationships and speaking with players in advance of a predictable milestone is invaluable," says Hall of Fame President Jeff Idelson. "The process starts months before, with written correspondence outlining our intentions. Meeting face to face with the player allows us to better articulate the enormity of the milestone, its relevance to the game's history and why it is important to have an artifact represented in the Museum."

Although the Hall of Fame is independent of Major League Baseball and its 30 clubs, the generosity of players, clubs and team personnel is important to the Museum's mission of documenting the game's history. According to Idelson players are, by and large, genuinely touched when asked to have an artifact in Cooperstown.

"Baseball players are 99 times out of 100 stunned to be asked for an artifact," he says. "Since I've been doing this, the players have held the Hall of Fame in tremendous esteem and feel honored when they're asked to contribute something."

Accessions Committee

BEFORE AN ARTIFACT THAT IS NOT TIME SENSITIVE IS ACCEPTED BY the Hall of Fame, it must be approved by the Hall's accessions committee.

Each month, the eight-person committee — made up of staff from collections, communications, curatorial, exhibits and the library — considers all baseball-related material for inclusion in the permanent collection. The committee must consider exhibition value, storage or display space, and condition and conservation concerns. Helpful in the process are photos, digital images, letters and accompanying information related to an item. Only after the group considers every factor and gives its approval are objects registered as artifacts and incorporated into the collection.

"We make sure we are really meeting our mission when we acquire something," says Jeff Idelson, who in addition to being the Hall's

President is an accessions committee member. "We turn down far more than we accept."

After being accepted by the Hall of Fame, each artifact gets its own number, which can be used to identify it as well as to track it as it's used outside the storage area.

"Everything is held in the public trust, so we have to take in only pieces we believe we can care for and exhibit to the public," says Sue MacKay, the Hall of Fame's director of collections and an accessions committee member.

Donations from fans may be tax deductible to the extent of the objects' market value. Donors get a lifetime pass to the Hall and a certificate of donation.

Fittingly, the House That Ruth Built was born on Feb. 6, 1921 — Babe Ruth's birthday. That was the day the Yankees announced the purchase of City Plot 2106, Lot 100, a 10-acre plot just across the Harlem River from Manhattan. Ruth, the 26-year-old outfielder who had just finished his first season as a Yankee, had proven to be such a drawing card that the Yankees were evicted from the Polo Grounds by their jealous landlords, the New York Giants.

The site was less than a mile from the Polo Grounds, but many thought the new stadium would struggle to draw fans due to its location. "Before long they will be lost sight of," Giants Manager John McGraw scoffed. "A New York team should be based on Manhattan Island."

After 185 days of construction, the stadium opened on April 18, 1923. As 74,217 fans streamed into the ballpark for that first game, workers still stood atop scaffolding, painting the outside facade. Some 25,000 people were denied admission that day, but those who did gain entry saw a baseball cathedral like nothing they had ever seen before. From the stately dark green seats to the gleaming copper frieze ringing the grandstand, it was the perfect setting for baseball history to be made. Ruth happily obliged, clouting the stadium's first home run in the bottom of the third — the first of 259 he would hit there before his career came to an end. To help commemorate the day, the Yankees distributed Opening Day pins, which can be seen at the Hall of Fame. Contrary to McGraw's prediction, the opening season in the Bronx was a resounding success. Although the stadium's first-year attendance of just more than 1 million was down slightly from their final three years at the Polo Grounds, it was head and shoulders above every other team in baseball.

JACKIE ROBINSON

INDUCTED IN 1962

JACKIE ROBINSON MADE his landmark debut in the Major Leagues in 1947, opening doors for fellow African-Americans in every walk of life.

"He struck a mighty blow for equality, freedom and the American way of life," United States President Ronald Reagan said after the Hall of Famer's death. "Jackie Robinson was a good citizen, a great man and a true American champion."

For several generations, no African-American baseball player had been allowed to participate in a Major League contest. Similarly, the state and local legislation collectively known as the Jim Crow Laws mandated segregation in most aspects of American society between 1876 and 1965. When legendary Brooklyn Dodgers General Manager Branch Rickey inked Robinson to a Minor League contract in 1945, the pair took bold steps toward undermining the prejudice that had buoyed an unjust way of life. A four-sport star at UCLA who excelled in the Negro Leagues, Robinson arrived at Ebbets Field after a brief stint with the Montreal Royals of the International League as the finished article — physically, emotionally and intellectually.

"He led America by example. He reminded our people of what was right, and he reminded them of what was wrong," American League President Gene Budig lauded. "I think it can be safely said today that Jackie Robinson made the United States a better nation."

"I SAID TO MYSELF MANY TIMES THAT I WASN'T GOING TO GET NERVOUS ON THIS OCCASION BUT HERE IT GOES AGAIN, THE SAME BUTTERFLIES I USED TO HAVE WHEN COMING UP WITH THE BASES FULL, BATTING AGAINST LEFTY GOMEZ OR LEFTY GROVE OR RED RUFFING. OF COURSE, IT MIGHT BE THAT THE NAME OF JOE McCARTHY BRINGS THESE TREMORS IN THE STOMACH. AND SEEING JOHNNY MURPHY OVER THERE, WATCHING HIM WARM UP IN THE BULLPEN AND KNOWING THAT PRETTY SOON HE'D BE IN THERE AND THROWING THAT CURVEBALL ON THE OUTSIDE."

HANK GREENBERG, JULY 23, 1956

Immediate Acquisitions

"BE PREPARED" IS NOT JUST THE MOTTO OF BOY SCOUTS, THE mantra also holds true for members of the National Baseball Hall of Fame and Museum's staff charged with acquiring artifacts from the most recent action on the diamond.

As baseball history can occur on any given day, Hall of Fame President Jeff Idelson and Senior Director of Communications and Education Brad Horn, both of whom worked for Major League clubs prior to joining the staff at Cooperstown, have often served as representatives of the Museum when pursuing artifacts from players and teams for both expected and unexpected achievements.

"If something like a no-hitter is pitched, it's an immediate phone call to the club requesting artifacts," Horn says. "If there's something arbitrary that requires a little more discussion, like the night that Stephen Strasburg struck out 14 batters in his debut [in 2010], it's a quick call to our senior director of exhibits and collections, Erik Strohl; a quick call to Tom Shieber, our senior curator; checking in sometimes with Jeff to say, 'Hey, does this have merit? Does this have a need for us to acquire?'"

One of Idelson's top memories harkens back to the day in 2004 when the Red Sox won their first title since 1918.

"I remember when the 2004 World Series ended in St. Louis," Idelson explains. "To me, one of the key pieces of their winning was the acquisition of Orlando Cabrera, because after he arrived and took over at shortstop he anchored their defense and then didn't commit an error in the postseason. So when I asked him for his glove, not only was he willing and humbled, but he gave me a huge hug. He couldn't believe it was coming to Cooperstown."

Authentication

AS THE AUTHORITY ON BASEBALL HISTORY, IT'S IMPERATIVE THAT the Hall of Fame and Museum not only authenticate its ever-growing collection of three-dimensional artifacts, but also do so thoroughly and with the utmost precision. According to Director of Collections Sue MacKay, the Museum doesn't authenticate objects for the public, but it does make every effort to verify all information about an artifact being considered for acquisition by using any available primary and secondary sources, including video and photo documentation.

"If it's from a recorded event, then we go to the source to try and match — let's say it's equipment — the look of the equipment to what we're seeing on the videotape or the photographs," MacKay says. "And we've done that quite a bit in the past — some have been successful, some have not."

When an object comes to the Hall from a fan, the Museum will try to get as much information as possible from the potential donor. While video and photos are used to verify the origin of recent items, if it's an item from an event that took place long ago, then a primary source — like a letter from a previous owner — is preferred.

"If we're not comfortable with the provenance of a piece, then we don't accept it," MacKay says. "It's very important that the public see material that has been fully researched."

About half of the roughly 400 three-dimensional artifacts that the Museum currently accepts annually come through the Major League Baseball Authentication Program. Launched in 2001, the initiative certifies artifacts with a numbered, tamper-proof hologram.

"Major League Baseball's authentication program has been very helpful," MacKay says. "They have a database online where you can match the number that's on the actual piece back to the list that they compile on their website. We're constantly checking it if pieces come in with that holographic sticker."

Museum Operations

THE WORD "MUSEUM" IS CERTAINLY A VITAL PART OF THE NATIONAL Baseball Hall of Fame and Museum, and as such the institution's head curator must deal with myriad issues on a daily basis.

For Erik Strohl, a given day includes a lot of communication with the two-dozen member staff in the four departments that report to him: curatorial, exhibits, library and collections. As the senior director of exhibitions and collections since April 2009, he says, "Really there's not a typical day. It's really helping about two dozen people do their jobs because everybody comes to me with whatever issues they're dealing with. Problem solving starts on my table. Whenever anyone has a need at the Museum that touches one of my four departments, it by necessity involves me. And it doesn't happen in order. It always seems to all happen at once."

It's not unusual for Strohl and his staff to have a month when they do their normal work but also take on a number of ancillary projects at the same time. "We work on our internal things, but we've also created eight exhibit cases full of 75 artifacts that we took to a trade show, hosted special VIP tours and the Library worked on a 1939 documentary.

"You've got to compartmentalize. I come in and say, 'What am I going to do today?' 'What am I going to do this week,' maybe, is the farthest I look ahead because otherwise I would never finish the list that I made. It would never be completely checked off."

As for the future, Strohl, who started his career at the Hall of Fame as an intern in 1998 and held various roles in the curatorial department before he accepted his current position as head curator, notes that the Hall must adapt with the times. "Every exhibit from here on out, we've got to talk about virtual connections," he says. "Web exhibits, mobile applications, iPod tours, how people can use their cell phones to interact. It's going to get wider and wider."

Collections Storage

WHILE THE NATIONAL BASEBALL HALL OF FAME AND MUSEUM counts tens of thousands of three-dimensional artifacts in its collection, only a small percentage are on display at any one time. The rest are housed in collections storage, not accessible to Museum visitors.

Artifacts housed here, all 2,675 square feet of it, are stored at a constant 68 degrees and 47 percent humidity. They are kept in movable storage units that condense the space in order to fit much more in an area than you would with stationary shelving.

"Environment is critical to the continued well being of any object, not just baseball material," says Director of Collections Sue MacKay. "I always stress to people that no matter what they're collecting, they need to make sure it's in a stable environment because the fluctuations in temperature and humidity and the exposure to light will damage any object."

The secure, climate-controlled repository protects the objects from light, dust, fluctuating temperature and humidity. In order to ensure that the material lasts forever, artifacts are stored in acid-free boxes and handled only when necessary, and then with white cotton gloves.

"Collections department staff is continually monitoring the condition of all materials," MacKay says. "Knowing the parameters of the materials is essential to mitigating the effects of time.

"Some materials, such as silk, are particularly fragile and will fade at a faster rate. Wool and cotton are stronger fabrics and hold up better over time. Polyester and nylon have different parameters and long-term effects are still unknown," she adds. "Early bats were made of hickory, rosewood, ash, etc. But maple has now entered the market and is being utilized by a growing number of players."

Security of the artifacts is also a high priority, with just a handful of staff members having access to the objects. Between the computer-coded swipe cards needed to open the door to the vault and the cameras positioned to see who is going in and out, potential problems have been mitigated.

"Once we accept something, we have to insure it and we need to make sure that it's preserved forever," MacKay says. "It's a big responsibility, but the public is trusting us to take care of the material that comes into the building. That's our job."

Following spread: Head Curator Erik Strohl (left) and Hall of Famer Andre Dawson at the Museum's Ted Williams strike zone display in 2010.

''BACK IN JANUARY, A FRIEND OF MINE PUT THIS WHOLE HONOR IN PERFECT PERSPECTIVE FOR ME. HE SAID 'MIKE, DO YOU REALIZE WHAT BEING IN THE HALL OF FAME MEANS? IT MEANS YOUR LIFE AND CAREER HAVE BEEN IMMORTALIZED. YOU'LL BE REMEMBERED FOREVER.' I SAID TO HIM, 'DOES THAT MEAN I'M IMMORTAL?' HE SAID, 'NO, MIKE. IT MEANS YOUR NAME IS IMMORTALIZED; THERE IS A DIFFERENCE.' WHEN I THOUGHT OF IT IN THAT WAY I HAD A GREAT NEW APPRECIATION FOR THE MAGNITUDE OF THIS WHOLE THING.''

MIKE SCHMIDT, JULY 30, 1995

STAN MUSIAL

INDUCTED IN 1969

ON SEPT. 17, 1941, with 12 days left in the season, the Cardinals called up an ex–Minor League pitcher who had recently become an outfielder. In those final weeks, the unheralded 20-year-old left-hander named Stan Musial established himself as perhaps the most successful September call-up in history, energizing the Cardinals with a .426 average and a .524 slugging percentage. Although St. Louis fell just short of the NL pennant, it was clear a star had been born.

Over the next five seasons, Musial led the Cardinals to four NL crowns and three World Series titles, establishing himself as the game's finest all-around player. He was a particular nemesis to fans of Brooklyn, St. Louis's greatest rival during the era. When Musial went 8 for 12 in a key 1946 series at Brooklyn's Ebbets Field, Dodgers faithful shouted "Here comes the man again!" whenever he strode to the plate. The nickname caught on, and from then on he was known as "Stan The Man."

He won three MVP Awards, but could have filled his shelf with many more. He batted as high as .376, hit as many as 20 triples and 39 homers, and drove in as many as 131 runs. His seven batting titles were the most since Ty Cobb's 11, and when he retired in 1963 he was the NL career leader in hits, runs, doubles and RBI. As great a player as he was, he impressed most people as a greater guy. Jovial, easygoing and beloved by all who met him, Musial was truly "The Man."

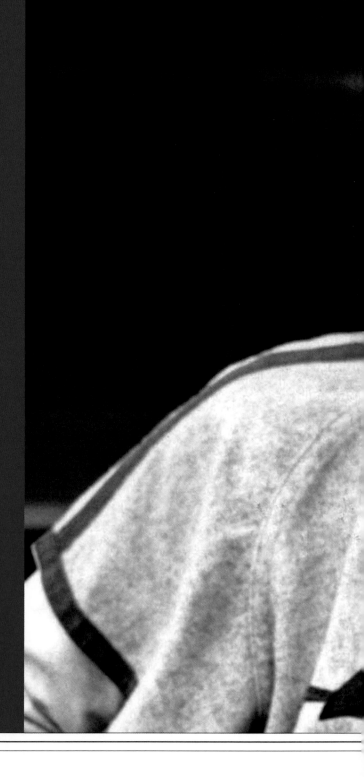

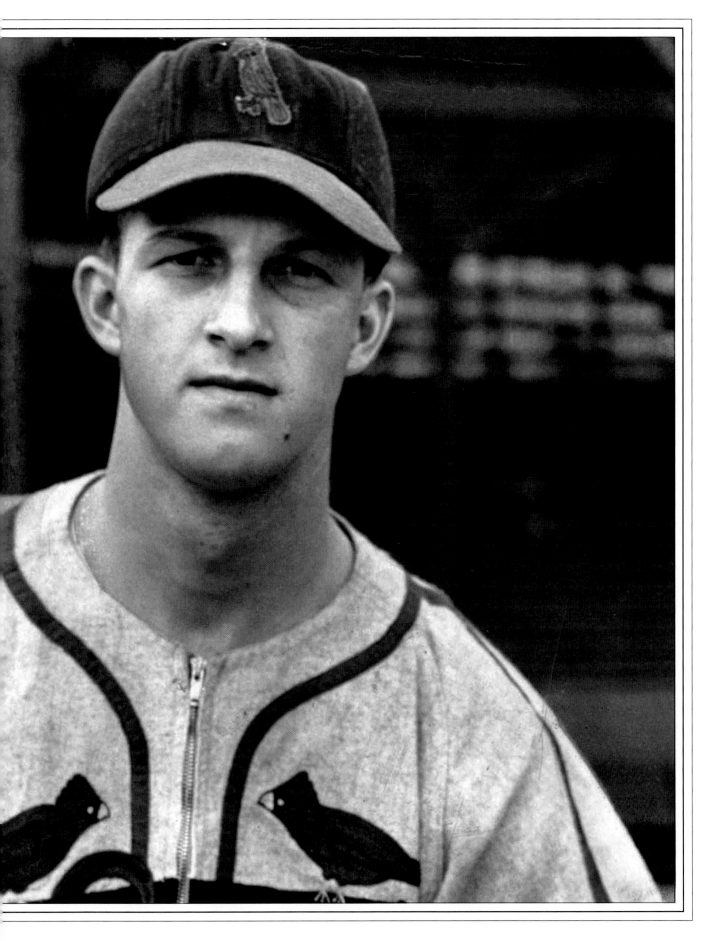

Chapter 4
Welcome to Cooperstown

TY COBB

INDUCTED IN 1939

FOR GENERATIONS OF fans who never had the privilege of seeing the Georgia Peach play, Ty Cobb's unparalleled achievements often have been overshadowed by the star's controversial and temperamental personality. Since his death in 1961, something approaching a new historical consensus has emerged. In Lawrence Ritter's classic book *The Glory of Their Times*, former teammate Sam Crawford depicted Cobb as an angry Southerner "still fighting the Civil War." Author Al Stump declared in his 1994 biography that Cobb suffered "acute self-worship" and "delusions of persecution."

There are plenty of incidents in Cobb's life that bolster such assertions. Quick-tempered and known to be violent, Cobb was also, like many Americans at the time, an unrepentant racist. But those now quick to judge Cobb as nothing more than brutal and self-centered would do best to take another look at this complex, fascinating figure.

Cobb made millions during his lifetime — mainly from investing in a fledgling soft-drink company in Georgia named Coca-Cola — and he donated much of his wealth to philanthropic causes. He established the Ty Cobb Memorial Hospital in his hometown of Royston, Ga., which provided members of the community with much-needed healthcare. He also established the Cobb Education Fund, which provided college scholarships to Georgia students lacking resources.

The Doubleday Ball

It may be hard to believe, but one old ball played a role in the National Baseball Hall of Fame and Museum calling Cooperstown, N.Y., its home. It all began one day in April 1935 when a farmer in Fly Creek, a crossroads village three miles from Cooperstown, came across a trunk in his attic that had gone untouched for generations. In the dust-covered case were the belongings of Abner Graves, who had grown up in Cooperstown a century before and was an ancestor of the trunk's discoverer.

Inside were a number of old items — books, pictures and an antique baseball unlike any seen today. The baseball, to a modern eye, was undersized, misshapen and obviously homemade. Its exposed interior was stuffed with cloth, rather than the tightly wound twine of the modern ball.

The locals had no doubt that the baseball had once belonged to Graves, who had testified later in his life that the game of baseball was invented in Cooperstown by Abner Doubleday. According to Graves, he was one of the schoolboys to whom Doubleday had taught the new game. It was therefore assumed that the baseball must have been handled by both Doubleday and Graves. It soon became known in the area as the "Doubleday Baseball."

Stephen C. Clark, a Cooperstown resident and philanthropist, purchased the baseball for $5 and placed it, along with other memorabilia, on exhibit in the Village Club, a building that sat on the corner of Main and Fair streets. With the financial support of Clark, the enthusiasm of the Cooperstown community and the official backing of Major League Baseball — notably National League President Ford Frick — plans to build a new museum to house the collection were announced in 1937.

After the Hall of Fame officially opened in 1939, the Doubleday Baseball — the first item accessioned by the Museum — was displayed for years on a mantle near a portrait of Doubleday. While much of the evidence Graves supplied about Doubleday's involvement in baseball has been proven incorrect, the ball remains one of the more popular and asked-about artifacts in the Museum's collection.

"Stephen Clark had great foresight in purchasing that baseball. It became a symbol for who we are and what our identity was and is," says Hall of Fame President Jeff Idelson. "It harkens back to the early days of baseball and it reminds us that the game was played in pastoral settings. It's a very poignant artifact."

The Doubleday Legend

Nestled in the heart of upstate New York, the village of Cooperstown boasts just a single traffic light amidst its 1.6 square miles and counts fewer than 2,500 year-round residents. So how did this sleepy hamlet become the home to the National Baseball Hall of Fame and Museum?

The easy answer to this common question is Abner Doubleday, a New York native who graduated from the U.S. Military Academy at West Point and eventually served as a Union General during the Civil War, taking a bullet while defending Fort Sumter and distinguishing himself on the battlefield at Gettysburg. For many years, the military hero was given credit for "inventing" the national pastime in Cooperstown.

It all begins with the Mills Commission, appointed in 1905 to determine the origin of baseball. During its three-year study, the committee was deluged with communications on the subject. The testimony in support of Doubleday by Abner Graves, a mining engineer then living in Denver, Colo., figured prominently in the committee's inquiry.

Graves claimed that he and Doubleday had attended school together in Cooperstown before Doubleday went off to West Point, where he graduated in 1842. In his letters to the Commission, Graves claimed to

have been present when Doubleday made changes to the popular game of "Town Ball," which involved 20 to 50 boys out in a field attempting to catch a ball hit by a "tosser" with a flat four-inch bat. According to Graves, Doubleday used a stick to mark out a diamond-shaped field in the dirt. His other refinements ostensibly included limiting the number of players, adding bases and the concept of a pitcher and a catcher.

The committee's final report on Dec. 30, 1907, stated, in part, that "the first scheme for playing baseball, according to the best evidence obtainable to date, was devised by Abner Doubleday at Cooperstown, N.Y., in 1839."

Having been given credit for devising the game of baseball, Doubleday's remarkable military service has been forever overshadowed. When the Hall of Fame building officially opened in 1939, *Time* magazine wrote: "The world will little note nor long remember what [Doubleday] did at Gettysburg, but it can never forget what he did at Cooperstown."

Almost immediately from the time the Mills Commission's results were announced, critics challenged the theory regarding Doubleday with their own well-documented evidence. Not only was Graves' credibility questioned, but Doubleday's diaries made no mention of baseball. To further complicate the situation, Doubleday was not away from

The Doubleday Ball.

West Point at all in 1839. There's even evidence that there may have been more than one Abner Doubleday.

Years later, it was Commissioner Ford Frick who intuitively said, "We make no claim that this, beyond all doubt, is the place where the first baseball game was played. But we do say that Cooperstown is the typical sort of American town where baseball could have first been played."

The likely truth is no one person invented the game, but it instead evolved from ball-and-stick games played many decades in various quiet towns before Doubleday was even born. According to Hall of Fame President Jeff Idelson, the question regarding Doubleday is no longer relevant to the institution.

"It was because of the Information Age that the realization that the Doubleday theory is a myth came about," Idelson says. "But by the time that happened, we had our own identity, so it wasn't quite a setback.

"It's a great story. Doubleday's a great character in American history because of his war efforts, and the Doubleday theory is important to understand from a historical standpoint. But by no means is it our current identity."

Doubleday Field

THE CITIZENS OF COOPERSTOWN APPRECIATED THE ACCLAIM THAT supposed baseball patriarch Abner Doubleday brought to their town, but they didn't find a suitable way to acknowledge it for years. When National League President John Tener came to Cooperstown in 1916, he visited a cow pasture that was once believed to have been used by Doubleday and other local boys to play the first game of baseball in 1839. Tener suggested that the pasture, owned by Elihu Phinney, be turned into a memorial to Doubleday. The townspeople soon acted on his advice.

Cooperstown hosted a summer-long series of events in 1939 — including the official dedication of the National Baseball Hall of Fame and Museum — to celebrate the centennial of the birth of baseball. In preparation for the numerous events, Doubleday Field underwent a facelift beginning in 1938, which included building a steel and concrete grandstand, installing new wooden bleachers, seeding the field, laying a drainage system, setting out a new board fence for the outfield and constructing stone masonry for the rest of the facility. These improvements would give the field a seating capacity of nearly 10,000.

Amazingly, the work on Doubleday Field was completed on the morning of May 6, 1939, the opening day of the Cooperstown Baseball Centennial. The first contest, which featured two upstate New York high schools, was just the first of more than a dozen the field hosted that summer. Most notable among them was a star-studded exhibition on June 12, after the first Hall of Fame Induction Ceremony, that featured ballplayers from every Big League team.

The All-Star affair in 1939 proved such a success that it prompted discussions of future tilts that would bring crowds back to Cooperstown during subsequent summers. Starting in 1940, the hugely popular Hall of Fame Game, an in-season exhibition between two Major League teams, would become an annual event that eventually saw such stars as Ted Williams, Mickey Mantle and Hank Aaron homer in Doubleday Field's hitter-friendly confines (296' to left, 336' to left-center, 390' to center, 350' to right-center, 312' to right).

Today, the fabled 9,791-seat ballfield, situated between Susquehanna, Pioneer, Elm and Main streets and surrounded in its idyllic setting with quaint houses and majestic trees, is not just a destination for baseball fans, but baseball teams from around the country. Owned and operated by the village of Cooperstown, Doubleday Field plays host to more than 350 baseball games every year, ranging from youth baseball to high school and collegiate tournaments to senior leagues. The village charges per game for the use of the field, with contests starting in mid-April and running through mid-October. Most of that time, the field hosts three games per day, seven days a week.

The Clark Family

NEARLY THREE DECADES AFTER THE MILLS COMMISSION'S REPORT, Stephen C. Clark, a Cooperstown native and heir to the Singer sewing machine fortune, unwittingly began to build the Hall of Fame.

"One day back around 1935, I was talking to Walter Littell, the local newspaper editor," Clark once said. "He mentioned that a man over in Fly Creek had found an old baseball and was offering to sell it. I bought it for $5."

That ball, dubbed the "Doubleday Baseball" because it was assumed to have been used by Abner Doubleday, was the impetus for Clark's involvement in the construction of a baseball shrine. Clark soon developed an

General Abner Doubleday. Following spread: Exterior of Doubleday Field.

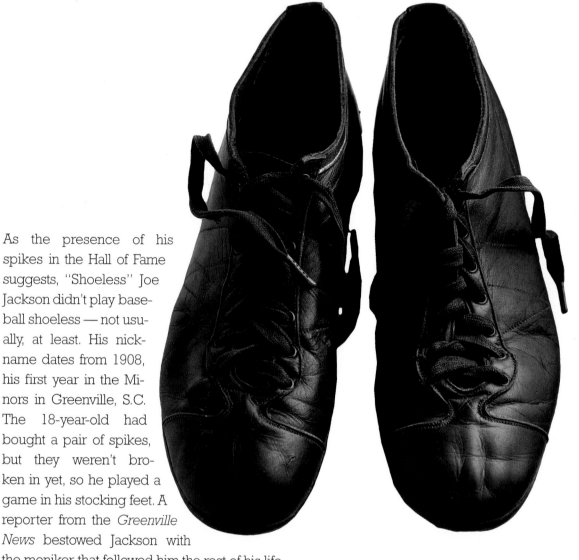

As the presence of his spikes in the Hall of Fame suggests, "Shoeless" Joe Jackson didn't play baseball shoeless — not usually, at least. His nickname dates from 1908, his first year in the Minors in Greenville, S.C. The 18-year-old had bought a pair of spikes, but they weren't broken in yet, so he played a game in his stocking feet. A reporter from the *Greenville News* bestowed Jackson with the moniker that followed him the rest of his life.

Jackson won the Carolina Association batting title that season, and by the end of the year he was in the Majors with Connie Mack's Philadelphia Athletics. The shy country boy had trouble fitting in on a club with so many college-educated players. Homesick, he lasted three days before fleeing to Greenville. He eventually returned, but batted .150 with the A's. In July 1910, convinced that Jackson would never adjust to Philadelphia, Mack traded him to the Cleveland Naps.

It was in Cleveland that Jackson came into his own. In six seasons with the Naps, he batted .375, including an MLB rookie-record .408 in 1911. Instead of slapping and bunting for hits like his Deadball Era peers, Jackson swung from the heels. In mid-1915, a blockbuster trade sent him to Chicago, where he continued to hit above .300 every season. But in 1919, resentful about his low salary, he accepted $5,000 to help throw the World Series to the Cincinnati Reds. Because he batted .375 in the Series, debate still rages about whether Jackson actually threw the games. However, he admitted accepting the money. When the scandal became public knowledge a year later, Jackson was banned from baseball for life — and from the Hall of Fame.

interest in collecting baseball artifacts. His original idea was to display the ball in the Cooperstown Village Club. But the ball soon attracted so much attention that he thought of establishing a baseball museum. Ford Frick, then the president of the National League, encouraged others to send their relics to Cooperstown and suggested to Clark in 1937 that he create a "hall of fame" to go along with the museum. Clark responded enthusiastically to Frick's suggestion and soon donated funds for the building, which officially opened in 1939. By the time Clark died in 1960 at age 78, he had served as president of the Hall of Fame since its dedication.

Four decades later, Clark's granddaughter, Jane Forbes Clark, was elected chairman of the Baseball Hall of Fame by the hallowed institution's board of directors. A Hall of Fame board member since 1992 and vice chairman beginning in 1993, she continues her family's leadership within the Hall of Fame.

"My family has cared very much for the Hall of Fame since founding it in 1939, and I look forward to continuing that stewardship," Clark said in response to taking on her new role. "Along with everyone on the Board, I look forward to the challenge of maintaining its integrity and world-class reputation. As the official repository for baseball's storied past, the Museum will continue to grow to meet the needs of baseball's passionate fans and be a place that connects generations."

Edward W. Stack, who Clark replaced as the Hall's chairman, added, "Unequivocally, she is the right person to be chairman of the Hall of Fame's board of directors and direct the Museum in the 21st century."

The First Class

AMAZING AS IT MAY HAVE SEEMED BACK THEN, BIG LEAGUE ACTION was shut down for a day as baseball's movers and shakers absconded to a small outpost in the Leatherstocking Region of Central New York that had been settled in 1786 by the father of famed American novelist James Fenimore Cooper. The picturesque village of Cooperstown had never seen a day like this and would change forever as a result.

Some 30 years after the Mills Commission had deemed the leafy community the original home of baseball, plans were underway for the village to host a four-month celebration in the summer of 1939, honoring the national pastime's 100th anniversary.

"Baseball has become, through the years, not only a great national sport, but also the symbol of America as the melting pot," wrote President Franklin Roosevelt in a letter earlier that year. "The players embrace all nations and national origins and the fans, equally cosmopolitan, make only one demand of them: Can they play the game?

"It seems to me that the museum will be a place of special interest, particularly in this centennial year of baseball."

From May through August of the year, Cooperstown was abuzz with baseball, with the newly christened Doubleday Field hosting special high school, college and semi-pro contests. The summer's crowning moment took place on Monday, June 12, a day that not only paid tribute to the game's best, but also marked the opening of a 1,200-square-foot shrine to the national pastime that fans from around the world enjoy to this day.

The Hall of Fame had been in the planning stages for a number of years before its official dedication and first Induction Ceremony. When the day finally came, crowds flocked to the historic village of 2,500 residents to witness the once-in-a-lifetime events that forever made Cooperstown part of the cultural landscape of our nation.

"My gosh, there were more people than cows," marveled Cooperstown resident Catherine Walker, who was just 8 years old at the time.

Approximately 12,000 fans, national press and three national radio broadcasters were in place at noon in front of the newly opened Hall of Fame on Main Street, where the 25 elected legends from the first four induction classes were to be honored with bronze plaques.

"Since for 100 years this game has lived and thrived and spread all over our country and a large part of the world, it is fitting that it should have a museum, a national museum," said Major League Baseball's first commissioner, Kenesaw Mountain Landis, at the beginning of the ceremony.

After a ruffle of drums, the sounding of taps was played for the 14 deceased inductees — Cap Anson, Morgan Bulkeley, Alexander Cartwright, Henry Chadwick, Charles Comiskey, Candy Cummings, Buck Ewing, Ban Johnson, Willie Keeler, Christy Mathewson, John McGraw, Charles Radbourn, A.G. Spalding and George Wright. Then the living honorees were introduced, and approached the microphone one at a time. All except Ty Cobb.

Connie Mack, Honus Wagner, Tris Speaker, Napoleon Lajoie, Cy Young, Walter Johnson, George Sisler, Eddie Collins, Grover Cleveland Alexander and Babe Ruth made short remarks for the crowd, the half dozen newsreel cameras and a nationwide radio audience, but the surly player known as the Georgia Peach was delayed because, according to reports, he was overcome with indigestion en route to Cooperstown and had to stop off at a hospital in nearby Utica.

"I was washing up over at Knox College," explained Cobb, "the only place in Cooperstown where I could get accommodations — when I heard my name read over the radio. I didn't know the ceremonies began that early.

"Called out on strikes, I guess," he laughed.

Evolution of the Hall of Fame

FROM HUMBLE ORIGINS — THE PLACING OF A BEAT-UP OLD BASEBALL in the Village Club — the National Baseball Hall of Fame and Museum has evolved into a world-class cultural showcase. During the ensuing decades, the Hall of Fame's mission to chronicle and preserve the story of our national pastime has inspired the institution to expand and embrace technology in search of bringing the game to more fans. Today the Museum is a must-see destination for baseball enthusiasts all over the world.

The Hall of Fame quietly opened its doors during the spring of 1938, a year prior to the official dedication. It all began as a two-story building with a couple thousand square feet of space. Today, its three floors total 127,000 square feet, split largely between public space (55,000), exhibit space (33,000) and the Library (37,000). In the original building's first floor, Hall of Famers' plaques were interspersed with artifacts, with the famed Doubleday Baseball occupying a place of honor on the fireplace mantle while a portrait of Abner Doubleday surveyed the scene.

Expansion and renovations completed in 1950 and 1958 enabled the Museum to display more of its growing number of artifacts and accommodate the increasing number of visitors. With students of the game needing better access to the Library's holdings that were located inside the Museum, a separate Library building was added in 1968. Further expansion and modernization took place in 1980, transforming the Museum's interior with state of the art technology.

"This expansion brought the exhibits and complex into the 21st century," said Edward W. Stack, the Hall of Fame's Chairman of the Board at the time.

While the *Timeline of Baseball History* was a focal point of the Museum, other notable exhibits included *Great Moments*, *Ballparks* and *Negro Leagues*. These new exhibits explored broader issues and marked a turning point in the Museum's presentation and philosophy.

The focal point of a 1989 expansion was the new Grandstand Theater, a 200-seat auditorium featuring a state-of-the-art multi-media presentation. During this time period, the Museum also opened the ground-breaking exhibit *Women in Baseball*. Even before the 1989 construction was complete, plans were underway for further modernization and expansion of the National Baseball Library.

The Museum also expanded its horizons with diverse new exhibits during this period. In 1995, *Baseball Enlists* highlighted the story of baseball's contributions to World War II. The following year marked the debut of the Perez-Steele Art Gallery, which featured paintings and sculptures. *Pride and Passion: The African-American Baseball Experience*, which opened in 1997, celebrated the history of black baseball from the Civil War era to Jackie Robinson's integration of the Majors to the accomplishments of current African-American stars.

The Hall of Fame's most ambitious renovation project was completed in 2005. Designed to add more gallery space, to be more accessible for those with special needs, and to incorporate more interactive technology, the Museum was entirely rededicated. Starting with that renovation, the Museum has opened nearly a dozen galleries in recent years, including *Taking the Field: The 19th Century*, *Diamond Dreams: Women in Baseball*, *¡Viva Baseball!* and *Hank Aaron: Chasing the Dream*.

Baseball Hall of Fame exterior in 1939.

"WE GOT THE SETTING — SUNSHINE, FRESH AIR. WE GOT THE TEAM BEHIND US. SO, LET'S PLAY TWO. I'M REALLY HAPPY AND HONORED TO SEE ALL THE MANY THOUSANDS OF CUB FANS HERE TODAY. THANK YOU VERY MUCH. I AM DEEPLY HONORED AND VERY GRATEFUL TO BE HERE TODAY. THIS IS CERTAINLY, AND IT WILL ALWAYS BE, THE HAPPIEST DAY OF MY LIFE."

ERNIE BANKS, AUG. 8, 1977

INDUCTION
SPEECH

LOU GEHRIG

ELECTED IN 1939

LOU GEHRIG WAS baseball's original iron man, earning him the nickname the "Iron Horse." The physically imposing Yankees first baseman suited up day after day for the better part of 15 seasons and, alongside Babe Ruth, imposed his will on the American League. In personality, Gehrig and Ruth were quite different. While Ruth actively sought the limelight, the humble Gehrig, more than eight years Ruth's junior, shied from it.

Born in Manhattan in 1903, Ludwig Heinrich Gehrig attended P.S. 132 in Washington Heights and then the High School of Commerce, on the Upper West Side, where his prowess on the gridiron won him a football scholarship to Columbia University. In his second year, he took to the baseball field. After seeing Gehrig at the plate in 1923, scout Paul Krichell wisely signed him to hit and play first base. By September, the 20-year-old Gehrig was in pinstripes as a late-season call-up.

Two years later, the regular first baseman, Wally Pipp, was suffering from a headache and Gehrig suited up. Pipp famously never got the job back. Gehrig hit better than .300 with 100-plus RBI for 12 straight seasons. "His shoulders were a yard wide and his legs looked like mighty oak trees," Hank Greenberg once said. "I'd never seen such sheer brute strength." Gehrig also set the mark for consecutive games played, at 2,130 (which remained unbroken until Cal Ripken Jr. topped it in 1995). In seven World Series, Gehrig was at his best, hitting .361 and adding six team titles to his already impressive resume.

Chapter 5
The Museum

PRIDE

& Passion

The African-American Baseball Experience

Pride and Passion

"THIS EXHIBIT IS DEDICATED TO THE MEN AND WOMEN WHOSE passion for our national game helped them triumph over obstacles brought about by prejudice and intolerance in our nation; and especially to Jackie Robinson, whose actions on and off the field served as the catalyst for progress, both in our game and in our society," reads the inscription dedicating the National Baseball Hall of Fame and Museum's exhibit *Pride and Passion: The African-American Baseball Experience.*

The 1,000-square-foot exhibit, located on the Museum's second floor, opened in 1997 to commemorate the 50th anniversary of Robinson's integration of Major League Baseball as a member of the Brooklyn Dodgers. It details the history of African-Americans in baseball, from the Civil War through the rise of the Negro Leagues and ultimately the integration of players, managers, scouts and executives at the Major League level.

"I think this is the final link," said Hall of Famer Joe Morgan at the exhibit's opening. "You can now go from Ty Cobb all the way up to Ken Griffey Jr. in this Museum and know exactly what you're talking about. Before there was an era missing. Now it's part of history and that's what it should be."

Pride and Passion breaks the story of African-American baseball from the 19th century to the present into six segments: Creating Opportunity (1860–87); Barnstormers (1887–1919); Separate Leagues, Parallel Lives (1920–33); Rebirth (1933–45); Changing Opportunities (1946–59); and Post-Integration (1959–present). Using artifacts, photos, audio and video, the exhibit chronicles the lives of many African-American pioneers in baseball history, such as Bud Fowler, Fleet Walker, Rube Foster, Jackie Robinson, Larry Doby, Buck O'Neil, Frank Robinson and Bob Watson. During the 1930s and early '40s some of the best players in any league were drawing large crowds in the Negro Leagues, including slugger Josh Gibson and pitcher Satchel Paige.

"This exhibit is not about artifacts," said then–Hall of Fame curator Ted Spencer at the exhibit's opening. "It's all about the story, and the story isn't over yet. It's still continuing. It's not just about the Negro Leagues; it's not just a Jackie Robinson exhibit. It's about 130 years of American history."

Notable artifacts in *Pride and Passion* include a Dodgers warm-up jacket, glove and bat used by Jackie Robinson; James "Cool Papa" Bell's St. Louis Stars jersey, cap and sunglasses; the Homestead Grays 1940 Negro National League championship trophy; a St. Louis Browns jersey worn by Paige in the 1950s; Hall of Famer Frank Robinson's uniform worn as a manager of the Cleveland Indians; and the 1949 Indians jersey worn by Doby, the first African-American player in the American League. The exhibit was entirely rededicated in 2004 to incorporate many fresh storylines and presentations.

Sacred Ground

BARRING THE INVENTION OF TIME TRAVEL, THE NATIONAL BASEBALL Hall of Fame and Museum's *Sacred Ground* exhibit is the closest a modern fan can ever come to taking in a ballgame in the storied parks of yesteryear. Opened in 2005 and located on the Museum's third floor, the exhibit covers 1,800 square feet and features more than 200 artifacts, a concession stand where children can act as vendors, integrated music and other interactive elements.

The popular exhibit focuses on six themes — Fans, The Stadium World, The Evolution of the Ballpark, Ballpark Business, Ballpark Entertainment and Reverence — each given their own distinct area within the exhibit. Ballparks of the past come to life in *Sacred Ground*, where an enormous 14-by-8 curved screen allows visitors to "walk-through" the Grand Pavilion at Boston's South End Grounds, which existed from 1888 to 1894. Chicago's Comiskey Park and Brooklyn's Ebbets Field are among the other bygone sights that this unique exhibit at the Hall of Fame revives.

"I love the exhibit. It brings back a lot of memories of parks I've been to or seen on television and in photos," says Liam Elliott, a fan from Des Moines, Iowa, who visited the Museum with his family. "This is the perfect place to remember the parks that are gone, and honor the parks we all love today."

Sacred Ground's artifacts include: the Comiskey Park scoreboard "pinwheel;" center-field padding from Tiger Stadium; a Forbes Field ticket box; a Wrigley Field "No Lights" placard; Walter Johnson's locker from Griffith Stadium; a microphone used by Bob Sheppard at Yankee Stadium; a metal season pass from the Palace of the Fans in Cincinnati; and a satin Boston Braves jersey used for night games at Braves Field.

Nicknamed "Spaceman," longtime Red Sox pitcher Bill Lee — known for his antics — may have been a symbol of the counterculture of the late 1960s but even he knew that ballparks were sacred. "You should enter a ballpark the way you enter a church," he once said. And, after exploring the *Sacred Grounds* exhibit fans will likely feel the same way.

Pride and Passion *exhibit. Following spread:* Sacred Ground *exhibit.*

LOWER
DECK
ROWS 26-47

LOWER
DECK
ROWS 1-25

TICKETS

CONCESSIO

DIAMOND DREAMS

Diamond Dreams

WOMEN HAVE PLAYED A SUBSTANTIAL ROLE IN THE HISTORY OF baseball — on the field as well as off. Fittingly, the National Baseball Hall of Fame and Museum has a space dedicated to telling the stories of women and their achievements on the diamond, in the press box and in the front office throughout the game's history.

The Museum dedicated a new exhibit titled *Diamond Dreams: Women in Baseball* on Mother's Day, May 14, 2006. Featuring artifacts dedicated to the wide variety of roles women play in baseball, the exhibit is an updated version of the popular display that first opened in 1988.

The *Diamond Dreams* exhibit features three main segments: "On the Field" focuses on stories of women competing in baseball, both professionally and in various amateur leagues; "In the Office" highlights the roles of female owners and executives; and "In the Stands" offers profiles of female fans, women who work in baseball as broadcasters, public address announcers and more, as well as the cultural impact of the 1992 film, *A League of Their Own*. An interview with Penny Marshall, the movie's director, is one of the many must-see items for visitors.

The exhibit's 85 artifacts include uniforms and equipment as well as photographs, text and multimedia. Notable items include a hardhat worn by Janet Marie Smith, a ballpark designer who oversaw renovations at Baltimore's Oriole Park at Camden Yards and the team's Spring Training venue Ed Smith Stadium in Sarasota, Fla.; a cap from Maria Pepe of Hoboken, N.J., whose landmark Supreme Court case in 1974 opened the door for young girls to participate in Little League; and a mask worn by Ria Cortesio, who in 2007 became the first woman to umpire a Big League exhibition game since 1989.

Life-Sized Statues

WALK IN AND AROUND THE NATIONAL BASEBALL HALL OF FAME and Museum and it's hard not to notice the life-sized statues. Whether sculpted from wood or bronze, they make an immediate impression. At one end of the Plaque Gallery stand Babe Ruth and Ted Williams sculpted in wood by Armand LaMontagne. Each slugger is captured in his batting stance and carved from a 1,400-pound block of laminated basswood. LaMontagne claims Williams broke down and cried upon first seeing his likeness when it was unveiled at the Museum in 1985.

The first permanent residents of the Hall's sculpture garden, located next to the Hall of Fame Library near Cooper Park, were life-sized figures of Brooklyn Dodgers pitcher Johnny Podres delivering a pitch to catcher Roy Campanella, who is stationed 60 feet, 6 inches away. Called "Eternal Battery Mates," the bronze sculpture captures the pair that led "Dem Bums" to victory over the Yankees in Game 7 of the 1955 World Series. It was originally meant for the Brooklyn USA Diner in Manhattan, but restaurant owner Sheldon Fireman, who commissioned the statues, had second thoughts.

"I felt they belonged in a place where more baseball fans could see them and appreciate them," Fireman says. "Then, when I met Baseball Hall of Fame Chair Jane Forbes Clark, it dawned on me. That's where they belong — in Cooperstown."

The pair of Brooklyn teammates, designed by Stanley Bleifeld, was donated to the Museum in 2001.

"I wasn't good enough to be enshrined in the Hall of Fame," Podres, who finished his career with a 148-116 record, once said, "but the statue is the next-best thing."

Other bronze statues by Bleifeld, including a female ballplayer and Negro Leagues star Satchel Paige, were erected in the outdoor venue in 2006. The first, made possible by a financial gift from Don and Chris Sanders of Houston and dedicated on Mother's Day, honored the contributions of women in baseball and the All-American Girls Professional Baseball League (AAGPBL).

"We wanted someone holding a bat," says former AAGPBL player Delores "Dolly" Brumfield White, "because everyone in the league got to take their turn at-bat."

Four more life-size statues were added in 2008, one being a smiling bronze John Jordan "Buck" O'Neil, created by sculptor William Behrends. He stands near the grand staircase on the Museum's first floor in front of engraved glass with quotes, descriptions and images of his baseball legacy, representing the Buck O'Neil Lifetime Achievement Award.

In November 2008, Behrends created three new pieces, which he called "Character and Courage" statues. The likenesses of Hall of Famers Roberto Clemente, Lou Gehrig and Jackie Robinson were unveiled in the Museum's lobby — a gift from Museum supporter Bob Crotty.

"The virtues they displayed on the field and in everyday life are inspiring," says Hall of Fame President Jeff Idelson about the trio.

Diamond Dreams exhibit. *Following spread: Life-sized statues of Lou Gehrig, Jackie Robinson and Roberto Clemente.*

CHARACTER AND COURAGE
Cast bronze by Stanley Bleifeld, 2008

Becoming a Hall of Famer takes more than just a great baseball career. Off-the-field challenges—and how those challenges are met—reveal an inner character that serves men and women throughout their lives. The life experiences of Lou Gehrig, Jackie Robinson, and Roberto Clemente stand out above all. Each faced personal and social obstacles with strength and dignity that set an example of character and courage for all others to follow.

Made possible through a generous donation by Robert Crary

NOLAN RYAN

INDUCTED IN 1999

NOLAN RYAN MUST have been a frightening foe to face during his high school days in East Texas. Armed with an incredible heater — and seemingly no idea of where it was going — he was said to have broken one opponent's arm and another's helmet on consecutive pitches. The New York Mets took a chance that Ryan could harness his power, and selected him in the 12th round of the 1965 amateur draft.

As a Minor League hurler, Ryan remained the prototypical gunslinger. "A guy either had the skill and timing to hit the heater, or he struck out," Ryan later said of the challenge he presented to batters.

Few were able to hit it, and by 1966 Ryan had kicked off his long and historic Big League career. He didn't stick around for so many seasons on speed alone, of course. Like numerous hard throwers before him, Ryan developed breaking pitches and became much better at locating his offerings, which allowed him to morph into a more complete pitcher.

He pitched for 27 seasons, becoming the game's all-time strikeout leader by a wide margin — the first to surpass 5,000, which he did with the Texas Rangers in 1989. In 1973, with the Angels, he threw his first of a Big League–record seven no-hitters. In 2 hours, 20 minutes that day, he issued three walks and struck out 12. Ryan could still light up the radar gun late in his playing days, thriving into his mid-40s while pitching for the Astros and Rangers in his native Lone Star State.

"I KNOW SOME FANS HAVE LOOKED AT 'THE STREAK' AS A SPECIAL ACCOMPLISHMENT, AND WHILE I APPRECIATE THAT, I ALWAYS LOOKED AT IT AS JUST SHOWING UP FOR WORK EVERY DAY. AS I LOOK OUT ON THIS AUDIENCE, I SEE THOUSANDS OF PEOPLE WHO DO THE SAME — TEACHERS, POLICE OFFICERS, MOTHERS, FATHERS, BUSINESS PEOPLE. YOU ALL MAY NOT RECEIVE THE ACCOLADES THAT I HAVE THROUGHOUT MY CAREER, SO I'D LIKE TO TAKE THE TIME OUT TO SALUTE ALL OF YOU FOR SHOWING UP, WORKING HARD AND MAKING THE WORLD A BETTER PLACE."

CAL RIPKEN JR., JULY 29, 2007

INDUCTION
SPEECH

A towering figure on the baseball landscape, Denton "Cy" Young was born in 1867, less than two years after the Civil War ended, and died in 1955, the year Rosa Parks refused to sit in the back of a Montgomery, Ala., bus. With a playing career that spanned an incredible 22 years, he also helped baseball evolve into the sport we know today. When Young first began pitching rural semipro ball in his native Ohio, the rules required pitchers to throw underhand. A walk was eight balls, and the pitching distance was just 50 feet. But by the time Young notched his record 511th win in 1911, baseball's rules were essentially the same as today.

Young's brilliant career was divided into two distinct halves. During the 1890s, with the NL's Cleveland Spiders, he whipped the ball homeward with such velocity that he won the moniker "Cyclone" (later shortened to Cy). But by 1900, injuries had rendered him ineffective on the mound. His owner declared him "all washed up," and many fans agreed. Signing with the up-start American League in 1901, however, provided a jolt to Young's career. He won the pitching Triple Crown that year, posted back-to-back 30-win seasons, led Boston to the inaugural World Series title in 1903, hurled a perfect game in 1904 and ended his Red Sox stint with 192 wins — which remains the franchise record. Not bad for a man whose career was supposed to have been over. His glove, on display in the Hall, represents his longevity and pitching excellence.

The Babe and The Hammer

Just two exhibits in the National Baseball Hall of Fame and Museum honor a single player. These two players — Babe Ruth and Hank Aaron — not only combined to top the career home runs list for more than eight decades, but are also two of three players ever to launch at least 700 home runs.

Although he played his last Big League game in 1935, Ruth remains one of the national pastime's most recognizable stars. The Babe Ruth Room, located on the Museum's second floor, has been in existence since the early 1950s and pays tribute to the man whose feats of power on the diamond inspired a new adjective — "Ruthian."

From his hardscrabble upbringing in Baltimore to his reign as the sport's brightest star, the exhibit employs photos, artifacts and a video presentation to teach visitors about George Herman "Babe" Ruth, both the player and the man. Among the exhibit's artifacts is a silver crown given to Ruth following the Yankees' 1921 World Series victory, decorated with 59 baseballs representing the new single-season home run record that he set that year; as well as the bat Ruth used to hit his legendary "called shot" home run during Game 3 of the 1932 World Series against the Chicago Cubs.

With power and panache in equal measure, the Bambino closed out the Deadball Era and instilled in fans a love of the longball that has endured until today. Not only was Ruth the first player to ever crack the 700-homer threshold, but he also set the bar high, besting many of his own batting records, not to be topped until Hank Aaron burst onto the scene nearly 20 years later.

The *Hank Aaron: Chasing the Dream* exhibit, located on the Museum's third floor and dedicated in 2009, chronicles Hammerin' Hank's life, from childhood through his Major League career and post-baseball activities, including his vast philanthropic efforts.

"No matter what you accomplish, what you achieve, you don't go down the path by yourself," Aaron said at the exhibit's dedication ceremony in April 2009. "I want to thank everyone who helped me along that path."

The first player to pass Ruth's seemingly unbreakable home run record, Aaron never had a 50-home run season. But his consistent pace — eight seasons with more than 40 longballs and another seven years with 30 or more — put him on pace to best Ruth's mark during the 1974 season.

"I don't want them to forget Babe Ruth," Aaron said to those critics who didn't want to see him break the Bambino's record. "I just want them to remember me!"

Artifacts in *Chasing the Dream* include the bat and ball used to hit home run No. 714 to tie Ruth's career mark; the bats and balls from his 3,000th hit, 500th and 600th home runs; the balls hit to record his 755th — and final — homer and his 2,210th RBI; the uniform shirt, pants, cap and helmet worn while he hit the record-breaking 715th homer; his locker from the former Atlanta–Fulton County Stadium; and his 1957 World Series ring.

"The artifacts need to be here so all people around the world can come see them," said Aaron, who donated many of the items himself. "I'm most comfortable with them here. It makes me feel proud."

Expansion and Renovation

The National Baseball Hall of Fame and Museum that opened its doors to the public for the first time in 1939 was a vastly different structure from the one that stands at 25 Main Street today.

Plans for the Cooperstown institution were first unveiled in July 1937, with Frank Whiting, a local architect, given the responsibility of designing the new structure. The two-story building had a Colonial design with walls made from James River Colonial brick and integrated with stone. The 1,200-square-foot first floor served as the plaque gallery, ticket office, museum, library, retail shop and director's office all in one, while the second floor stored library materials.

In 1946, the architectural firm of Harry St. Clair Zogbaum drafted plans to double the size of the facility. The $175,000 addition to the

west side of the original structure increased exhibit space and created a new entrance. It was dedicated on July 24, 1950.

The new Plaque Gallery, a chapel-like structure built of brick and steel with Vermont black marble columns supporting a lofted ceiling, was dedicated eight years later, on Aug. 4, 1958. A decade later, a building to house the expanding Library was built in Cooper Park, next to the Museum, and was dedicated on July 22, 1968, in conjunction with that year's Induction Ceremony.

"In the 1950s, we really began to realize that we were two institutions under one roof — a Hall of Fame, where we honored the all-time greats, and a Museum, where we told the history of baseball," says Howard Talbot, the former director of the Hall of Fame. "We needed to

Following spread: Hank Aaron: Chasing the Dream exhibit.

build a gallery to make that distinction and accommodate the growing number of elected members."

With attendance on the rise, the Hall of Fame completed its fourth expansion in 1980. The three-year, $3 million project included the construction of a west wing attached to the 1950 addition, which mirrored the original building and added symmetry to the overall appearance of the structure from the street entrance.

In 1989, a new wing was added. The $7 million project, dedicated as the Fetzer-Yawkey Building, was the fifth major expansion in 50 years. John Fetzer, then chairman of the board of the Detroit Tigers, and Jean Yawkey, then chairwoman of the corporation that owned the Boston Red Sox, each made significant contributions to the project.

In the early 1990s, the Library added 22,000 square feet to the original 7,000-square-foot building, in the form of a research area, exhibit gallery, bookstore, theater, state-of-the-art storage facility and curved hallway that connected the Library to the Plaque Gallery.

"After 25 years, the expansion physically connected the Museum and Library once again," said former Baseball Hall of Fame Librarian Tom Heitz. "We wanted to encourage visitors to take advantage of all of the Library's resources."

The most recent renovation, completed during the spring of 2005, focused on enhancing existing space rather than expansion. Designed by Hugh Hardy, the $20 million project tied all existing structures together, creating a flow from one gallery to the next. The project also improved access to the Museum for those with special needs, and furthered the institution's artifact preservation capabilities. As a result of its improvements, the Hall of Fame boasts several unique structures, built over a 70-year span, to house its extensive collection.

Grandstand Theater

ALTHOUGH ITS FACILITIES HAVE PERIODICALLY UNDERGONE improvements during the past two decades, one of the National Baseball Hall of Fame and Museum's favorite attractions has not lost the charm that made it so popular in the first place.

Designed to resemble old Comiskey Park, the 200-seat Grandstand Theater first opened its doors in 1989 to coincide with the Hall of Fame's 50th anniversary, and is still a must-see stop for visitors. Over the years, millions of fans have been drawn to its stirring multimedia presentation called *The Baseball Experience*. The presentation originally relied on multi-image technology, in which 18 slide projectors worked in synch with film and video projectors.

In 2003, thanks to the funding help of the Yawkey Foundation, the Hall of Fame modernized the facility. Today the presentation is done with computer software and a system involving three digital, high-resolution video projectors. Images from the three projectors are blended seamlessly on the 9-by-27 screen, making the entire thing almost new to those who had seen it in the past.

When the Grandstand Theater first opened, then–Hall of Fame Vice President Bill Guilfoile recommended that visitors see the theater show before exploring the premises, as a "nice orientation." Nothing has changed, as it's designed not so much to be a historical piece, but rather to get people to start thinking baseball.

The Grandstand Theater screens its 13-minute show, *The Baseball Experience*, every 20 minutes during the summer months and every hour throughout the rest of the year.

"There are parts of the show that everyone who has ever played baseball can relate to," says Bruce Brodersen, Hall of Fame director of multimedia. "The only complaint I've heard about it over the years is that it's too short."

The Babe Ruth Room. *Following spread: The Grandstand Theater.*

Chapter 6
Knowledge and Education

When Ted Williams lofted a home run to center at Fenway Park in his last Big League at-bat on Sept. 28, 1960, there was little doubt that he was the game's best pure hitter. With a 1-for-3 outing in his final game, Williams finished the 1960 season with a .316 average. What may have been a career-year for many was actually the second-worst season-long average for the player who had hit .406 in 1941.

Williams collected two Triple Crowns and remains the last Major Leaguer to record a .400 or better batting average in a season. Not surprisingly, one of his bats made its way to Cooperstown along with Williams, who was inducted in 1966.

"I remember holding a Ted Williams bat. That was a really neat thing," Twins backstop Joe Mauer, no stranger to the batting crown himself, says of a rookie season trip to Cooperstown. "I was always a big fan of Ted Williams because he was my grandpa's favorite player. I had a real close relationship with my grandpa growing up. He'd always talk about Ted Williams. We got to do a lot of neat stuff in the Hall of Fame, but holding Ted Williams' bat probably meant a little more because he was my grandpa's favorite."

Hitting was both an art and a science for the perennial MVP candidate, who perfected the task in his 19-year career in Boston. And in Cooperstown, even Big Leaguers like Mauer are awestruck by the Splendid Splinter's weapon of choice.

The Library

Whether you're trying to track down the box score from the first Big League game you ever attended, an old photo of a favorite but long-forgotten player or some unique version of "Take Me Out to the Ball Game" that you remember from a film, there's only one place where you're nearly guaranteed to find an answer.

The Baseball Hall of Fame Library, the country's largest and most comprehensive sports library, is a one-stop destination for all inquiries about the national pastime. The Library's staff is peppered with upwards of 100,000 questions a year from colleagues within the Hall and those outside the institution via phone, letters, fax, e-mail and walk-in users.

The Library's mission is to collect and preserve baseball's rich history, while making it accessible to the public. It began in 1939 with 400 books and documents on a few shelves on the Hall of Fame's second floor. An advertisement in *The Sporting News* that year appealed for donations: "Help Enshrine the Game's History! Contributions Wanted for the Baseball Library Now Being Established by the National Association at the Baseball Museum — at Cooperstown, N.Y. Baseball Books — Old Contracts — Manuscripts and Any Other Documents of Historical Value Relating to the Development of the Game and Its Leading Figures."

Today, the 37,000-square-foot Library, with its two floors, basement and six climate-controlled storage rooms, contains about 3 million items, including 500,000 photographs, 20,000 books, 14,000 hours of recorded media, 25,000 clipping files containing more than 1 million clippings, and another million documents still to be cataloged.

"We preserve the documented history of baseball, and not just Major League Baseball but all material related to the game's history," says Jim Gates, the librarian at the Hall of Fame. "As an educational institution, we use our collection to teach about baseball, but we also use baseball to teach other topics. And there are not topics that I've come across yet where we can't teach using baseball as a foundation piece."

Having outgrown its original space in the Hall of Fame building, the Library moved in 1968 to a new structure in Cooper Park across from a statue of the local novelist James Fenimore Cooper. This was a fresh development in sports scholarship — a game with its own library.

"We are here after years of work," former MLB Commissioner Ford Frick said at the time, "to dedicate the only library that has been built by sports people for sports people."

From its beginning, the Baseball Hall of Fame Library has been *the* repository for all baseball-related information, including team documents, historical records and individual clippings on file for each of the 17,000-plus men who have played in the Big Leagues, as well as files for most Negro Leagues and women's leagues players and countless Big League owners, umpires, broadcasters, executives and other baseball personalities. Visitors will also find baseball books, magazines, scrapbooks, photographs from the morgues of now defunct New York City newspapers the *World-Telegram*, *Herald Tribune* and *Journal-American*, rule books, scorecards, oral histories, stamps, game programs and player questionnaires.

"Everybody from a third-grader with a homework project to a Ph.D. candidate working on a dissertation, game shows like *Jeopardy!* and *Who Wants to be a Millionaire?* looking to verify a question, both broadcast and print media, team executives, baseball public relations departments, player agents, players' families, fans, authors, a patron at a bar with a $20 bet riding on a question," Gates says about the broad spectrum of visitors the Library attracts on a regular basis.

"When the phone rings, you never know who's going to be on the other end. If the president of the United States is going to use baseball in a speech, the White House speechwriting office will call us to confirm that the information is correct."

A statement from *The Otsego Farmer*, a Cooperstown-area newspaper, when the new building housing the accumulated knowledge of the national pastime first opened in 1968, may still hold true today:

"The library is a tremendous addition to the history, legend and lore of the great national game. It will prove its worth and usefulness a thousand times over in the years to come."

The A. Bartlett Giamatti Research Center

There's no dress code at the National Baseball Hall of Fame, and fans often show up wearing apparel touting their favorite team, but there is one public area where white cotton gloves are required.

Housed within the Hall of Fame Library — its entrance just inside the bookstore on the first floor — is the A. Bartlett Giamatti Research Center, which opened in 1968. The room was dedicated 30 years later to honor former Commissioner A. Bartlett Giamatti, who had invested much in the Library before he passed away in 1989. The center's collections include, among other things, books; periodicals; two-dimensional paper items; clipping and photograph files; and film, video and recorded sound collections.

Following spread: The Library's exterior.

"Our job is to provide baseball information to people who are looking for it," says Director of Research Tim Wiles. "Our customers include everyone from the public and the media to our own organization, which can include public relations, the retail department and the curatorial staff."

Hanging on a wall, looking down on those researching the game, is a 1967 painting of Hall of Fame skipper Casey Stengel donning a New York Mets uniform. An apropos message beneath the painting reads: "As Casey once said … 'You could look it up.'"

The Giamatti Research Center is a closed stack library, requiring researchers to request materials from the reference desk. In order to help preserve documents and artifacts, researchers are then required to wear white gloves provided by the Library when examining any materials.

Despite such precautions, accessibility is important at the Research Center, which welcomes everyone from curious walk-in visitors to well-known authors who spend weeks digging deep into the archives.

"People use the Research Center in two ways," explains Wiles. "People who have bought a ticket to the Museum can just drop into the Research Center and ask a question and we'll do our best to answer it quickly. People also make appointments for the Research Center to do longer term research for things like a book, a film or a college paper."

The multi-part documentary *Baseball* by Ken Burns owes much to the Hall of Fame. Similarly, famous baseball chroniclers such as Roger Kahn, George Plimpton and Roger Angell have enriched their works thanks to the Research Center. Films such as *A League of Their Own*, *The Natural*, *Field of Dreams*, *Eight Men Out*, *Frequency* and *61** and television programs ranging from *Dr. Quinn, Medicine Woman* to *The X-Files* also have benefitted from the vast resources available at the research center.

But sometimes it's the small, personal moments that remain the most memorable for the staff. Finding a relatively arbitrary artifact can be deeply meaningful for a visitor.

"People will come in and say, 'My dad took me to my first game in 1938 or 1939, and I remember Mel Ott hit a home run, and it was on a Saturday,'" Wiles says. "We'll go check the schedule, find the box score of the game and give the person a copy of it. And they go away with tears in their eyes. Happens all the time."

Hitting the Books

AS THE DIRECTOR OF RESEARCH AT THE BASEBALL HALL OF FAME Library, Tim Wiles has helped countless fans over the years with inquiries when it comes to the national pastime. Much like a grizzled detective, he knows exactly how and where to track down just about any answer, no matter how obscure the question. When trying to solve a baseball mystery, though, there are a few particularly trusted guides at the Hall's A. Bartlett Giamatti Research Center that Wiles frequently goes to for the answers.

According to Wiles, Peter Morris's *A Game of Inches: The Stories Behind the Innovations That Shaped Baseball* is "a true baseball encyclopedia. You can look up virtually anything about baseball, not just statistics, and get a sense of how that rule, custom, tradition or practice developed and why."

Another favorite go-to source for the Hall's top researcher is *Professional Baseball Franchises: From the Abbeville Athletics to the Zanesville Indians*, by Peter Filichia. The unique book is comprised of an alphabetical list of every single professional baseball team of all time. "You can find out here in this book the years of existence for each franchise, as well as, most entertainingly, the team's nickname," says Wiles. "My favorite is the Greenville (Miss.) Swamp Angels, who existed only in the 1923 Cotton States League, Class D. Additional research on my part has indicated that 'swamp angel' is actually a local euphemism for mosquitoes."

Although Wiles admits that Dan Gutman's offbeat and sometimes humorous *Banana Bats and Ding-Dong Balls: A Century of Unique Baseball Inventions* "seems to have been written in order to entertain," he does give it credit for being "one of the only one-volume histories of baseball equipment."

But Wiles' list of favorites includes just a few of the volumes of baseball research literature that can be found on the vast shelves of the Hall of Fame Library. Author Paul Dickson explores the use of different baseball terminologies in two of the works that he has contributed to the collection. For questions regarding the sport's lingo — ranging from slang terms and fantasy baseball expressions to phrases introduced by foreign-born players — turn to *The Dickson Baseball Dictionary* and its 10,000-plus entries. To see these phrases put to use by some of baseball's most charismatic personalities from all eras, *Baseball's Greatest Quotations*, a compilation of more than 5,000 unforgettable comments on the sport, is yet another useful tool in the library's collection.

Possibly the most comprehensive of all research guides is Myron J. Smith's *The Baseball Bibliography*, a massive undertaking that compiles the history of baseball into four volumes that have been touted as the largest American print bibliography chronicling *any* sport. Hardball enthusiasts can spend days scouring the volumes for information on any baseball inquiry.

To win the World Series, it certainly helps to have a superstar like Mickey Mantle or Derek Jeter on your team — but it's vital to have players like Scott Brosius as well. A hard-nosed player whose uniform always seemed to be dirty, Brosius helped spark the Yankees to three world championships between 1998 and 2002.

He was a decidedly unlikely hero. In seven years with the Oakland Athletics, Brosius posted an on-base percentage better than .300 just twice. His main value was not his bat, but his defensive versatility. In 1995, for instance, he played three or more games at each of seven different positions. In '97, though, after a dismal .203 performance at the plate, the Athletics released him. Catching on with the Yankees, he enjoyed a career year as the team won 114 games in 1998. Brosius not only hit .300 and drove in 98 runs, but also contributed a game-winning three-run homer in Game 3 of the World Series.

In 2001, he was at it again. Entering Game 5, Brosius was batting just .231 in the Series. But New York was riding high after Tino Martinez hit a game-tying homer with two outs in the ninth, sparking an unlikely comeback win in Game 4. Remarkably, the same thing happened in Game 5, but this time it was Brosius who played the part of hero. With the Yankees once again down to their last out of the game, Brosius smacked a game-tying two-run homer off Arizona's Byung-Hyun Kim, and his bat, pictured here, now resides in Cooperstown. The Yankees won it three innings later, and Brosius was the toast of New York. "One of the strengths of our team is that we play hard for 27 outs," Brosius said after the game. "You don't want to make your living waiting until the 26th out to make something happen, but it has worked the last two nights."

FRANK ROBINSON

INDUCTED IN 1982

FRANK ROBINSON FIRST garnered attention at Oakland's McClymonds High School, where, along with team-mates Curt Flood and Vada Pinson, he was part of what may have been the best high school outfield ever. The three would eventually play a total of 54 Big League seasons and collect 7,561 hits (led by Robinson's 2,943). In high school, Robinson also played basketball alongside future Boston Celtics legend Bill Russell — and, of course, led the team in scoring.

Once in the Majors, Robinson turned to pacing the Big Leagues with his bat. And as a base runner, he gained a reputation as the most aggressive and fearless in the sport, in particular for his tendency to try to break up double plays. "If you can't break up a double play, knock the man down anyhow," he said in 1963. "Make him think a little the next time you come around."

But as much as Robinson's opponents may have feared him, his teammates revered him. He was the undisputed leader of the Orioles: league MVP, judge of the Kangaroo Court and paternal figure to young players such as Davey Johnson, Bobby Grich and Don Baylor.

Whispers began as early as 1963, when Robinson was 27, that he would eventually become baseball's first African-American manager. Finally, on Oct. 4, 1974, Robinson was introduced as the player-manager of the Cleveland Indians, making him the first African-American manager in Major League Baseball history. He hit a homer in his first game as his own skipper.

"WHERE DO YOU START? WHERE CAN YOU POSSIBLY START? TO FEEL THE EMOTION, WHERE CAN YOU POSSIBLY START TO SAY THE WORDS THAT WILL EXPRESS WHAT HAS TAKEN PLACE IN A MAN'S LIFE OVER A 20-YEAR PERIOD AND BEYOND? FOR ME, IT'S THE LAST BEAUTIFUL FLOWER IN THE PERFECT BOUQUET BECAUSE THE 20 YEARS THAT I HAD AS A PROFESSIONAL ATHLETE PLAYING FOR THOSE FOUR WONDERFUL TEAMS AND THAT 20-YEAR PERIOD BEFORE MY PROFESSIONAL CAREER BEGAN ALL CAME TOGETHER FOR ME IN THIS INDUCTION IN THE HALL OF FAME."

TOM SEAVER, AUG. 2, 1992

INDUCTION
SPEECH

115

Photographs

APPROXIMATELY 500,000 MOMENTS, CAUGHT IN TIME FROM baseball's long and varied history, are currently stored in Cooperstown at the National Baseball Hall of Fame and Museum.

Located in the basement of the building housing the Hall of Fame Library, the 922-square-foot photographic collection archive is housed in a climate-controlled vault kept at a steady 59 degrees Fahrenheit with 26 percent humidity, conditions ideal for preservation. Rows upon rows of hanging folders of photographs are located on movable storage units in the vault. Not only are there photo files for a majority of the 17,000 players who have played Big League ball since the 1860s, but the collection also includes files on stadiums, teams, tours abroad, All-Star and postseason games, Hall of Fame events, and many other subjects.

The Hall's collection, which has continually expanded throughout its history, consists primarily of black and white prints, but also includes color photographs, film and glass negatives, slides and an increasing number of digital images. A print donated in 1937 by Hall of Famer Clark Griffith depicting President Warren Harding opening the Senators' 1921 season was the first photograph accessioned into the Hall's collection. Since the donation of that first image, the stock has grown immensely.

The photo archive, assembled entirely through donation, is composed of images from a number of sources, including Major League clubs — in the form of publicity shots — news and wire services, baseball card manufacturers and fans. The Hall has also acquired personal collections from current and former players and their families, journalists, photographers and collectors over the years.

An important part of the collection has come from the photography archives of three former New York City newspapers: the *World-Telegram and Sun*, the *Herald Tribune* and the *Journal-American*. Although the trio of papers merged in 1966, the resulting publication went out of business soon after (in 1967), and the approximately 30,000 baseball images that had been saved by the newspapers since their early days as individual publications arrived in Cooperstown the following year for preservation.

Today, the half a million or so photos in the Library basement collection are available to the public for research, publication, exhibition and personal use — copies of the photos can be made and serve as unique souvenirs for visitors. The images are also incorporated into the museum's numerous exhibits.

Recorded Media

ALSO LOCATED IN THE BASEMENT OF THE BASEBALL HALL OF Fame Library is the Recorded Media Department, where more than 14,000 hours of audio-video material on various analog video formats (from BetaSP to VHS and 1-inch), film (8, 16, and 35 mm), vinyl 45s, 78s, LPs, 1/4-inch tape, cassettes, micro cassettes, cylinders, CDs and DVDs are stored.

"The recorded media collection reflects the institution's goal of acquiring the widest variety of material reflecting how baseball has become an integral part of our society and culture," says Librarian Jim Gates.

Among the media collection's highlights is one of the earliest recordings of baseball's signature tune, "Take Me Out To The Ball Game," on an Edison cylinder. Although it has since been recorded more than 500 times by various artists, Jack Norworth and Albert Von Tilzer's original song has not waned in popularity since its early days, more than 100 years ago.

And the recording doesn't just collect dust in the basement. In 2008, the Hall of Fame hosted an electronic field trip — an initiative that typically reaches 10 million students or more — featuring the song, conducted through interactive distance learning technology. Filmmaker Ken Burns collected more than 200 different recordings of the song for use in his documentary *Baseball*.

Also included in the Recorded Media Department are a collection of original acetate discs of broadcasts from baseball games from 1934 through 1945; Commissioner Kenesaw Mountain Landis's collection of off-air aluminum disk recordings of All-Star and World Series games from the 1930s; and Lawrence Ritter's original reel-to-reel interviews for his classic book *The Glory of Their Times*. Over the past several decades the Recorded Media Department has also been able to assemble an impressive collection of baseball oral history interviews, which now number more than a thousand.

"These interviews have not only been recorded by our own staff," Gates says, "but by members of the Society for American Baseball Research (SABR) Oral History Committee, academic researchers and book authors, helping to make it one of the most significant sports oral history repositories in the nation."

Photo collection storage.

The Hall of Fame Librarian

"Every morning I have a written plan of the day, and by 9:30 a.m. it has changed."

According to Baseball Hall of Fame Librarian Jim Gates, flexibility is the most important skill to have for his job. Since 1995, Gates has overseen the Research, Reference, Photo, Recorded Media and Technical Services departments and the use of more than 3 million items that make up the collections of the Library.

Much of Gates' work focuses on the acquisition and presentation of the Library's collections, but encouraging the donation of items that document baseball history is another big part of his job. He has been very active in getting noted authors, including Jules Tygiel, Roger Kahn, Roger Angell and Robert Creamer, to donate their manuscripts and research notes — many of which were compiled in the Hall's Library and the Giamatti Research Center.

"I'm constantly being surprised," Gates says. "I don't know what's going to come in the mail."

One day Gates' mail included a collection of love letters from a ballplayer, another day a packet of material on a play about Casey Stengel that was put on in New York.

When Gates is asked what his favorite baseball publication is, his answer is always the same: "My favorite baseball book is the one I need to answer the next question," he says. "And after that, when another baseball question comes in, I have a new favorite baseball book. I view them as tools that I need to do my job."

Gates embraces the opportunities to present all of the Library's collections through exhibits, staff research, public research or online. And with the Hall of Fame exploring the diverse presentation opportunities that have emerged with new technologies, future possibilities are endless.

Education

Designed to serve kindergarten through 12th-grade audiences, the National Baseball Hall of Fame's Education Department is busy throughout the year, but it's during those months when school is in session that the place is buzzing with activity.

Whether it's taking field trips to Cooperstown or bringing the Hall of Fame to the classroom through videoconferences — teachers can select a themed unit and participate in an interactive lesson led by an educator — the Hall's message has been consistent since the programs began in 1991.

"Our goal is to make sure students experience the Baseball Hall of Fame in a meaningful way, but also that they learn as much as they can without realizing that they're learning," says Director of Museum Education Anna Wade. "We use baseball as a hook to introduce concepts that are already being introduced in classrooms all over the country."

The Hall of Fame offers 16 learning modules ranging from Science on the Sandlot to Character Education: Lou Gehrig — the Iron Horse to Women's History: Dirt on Their Skirts. The Education Department hosts approximately 100 school groups (about 7,000 students) and 500 videoconferences (about 25,000 students) each year, teaching civil rights, geography and communication, among other topics, through the prism of baseball.

"The goal is to have students take the knowledge they already have and make a connection here at the Museum," Wade says. "And not everybody can get to Cooperstown, so a distance learning program, the EBBETS (Electronically Bringing Baseball Education to Students) Field Trip Series, has been designed to allow live videoconferences with students all across the country."

"There used to be a ballpark where the field was warm and green," Frank Sinatra sang in a 1973 song, "and the people played a crazy game with a joy I've never seen." The ballpark he was singing about was Ebbets Field, the cozy, creaky, dilapidated and beloved home of the Brooklyn Dodgers from 1913 to 1957. Appropriately enough for the hapless team known as "Dem Bums," the stadium was built on the former site of a garbage dump and its official opening day on April 9, 1913, was delayed because team officials forgot to bring the key to open the bleachers. They also forgot to build a press box or bring an American flag.

No matter how bumbling the team could be, Brooklynites loved their ballpark almost as much as their Dodgers. They weren't deterred by the franchise's seven straight World Series losses between 1916 and 1953. Ebbets Field was, as Jackie Robinson's widow, Rachel, told it to the New York *Daily News*, "a small, intimate place where everybody knows everybody."

By the mid-1950s, though, fewer fans were attending games. Ebbets was in decline, and with their proposed new ballpark in Brooklyn rejected, the Dodgers opted to move to Los Angeles. The move wasn't made official until October 1957, but the writing was on the wall by the last game at Ebbets Field, on Sept. 24. Fans didn't care about a team that was no longer theirs, and a crowd of just 6,702 showed up to witness Brooklyn's last gasp in the Majors. Those who counted themselves among the Flatbush Faithful can still see relics, like the seats from Ebbets Field, at the Hall of Fame.

"I'M GOING TO TELL A LITTLE STORY FIRST ABOUT A COUPLE OF FRIENDS WHO ARE SUPPOSED TO BE TRUE YANKEES AND [WERE] ABSOLUTELY THRILLED THAT I MADE THE HALL OF FAME AND SAID I DID THEM PROUD: YOGI BERRA AND WHITEY FORD. AT THE HALL OF FAME LAST NIGHT, I ASKED YOGI, I SAID, 'YOGI, DO YOU THINK I COULD HAVE PLAYED FOR THE YANKEES WHEN YOU PLAYED?' YOGI SAYS, 'I DON'T KNOW REGGIE.' I WAS TALKING TO ELSTON HOWARD AND HE SAID, 'YOU MIGHT BE OUR FIFTH OUTFIELDER.'"

REGGIE JACKSON, AUG. 1, 1993

Chapter 7
Outreach

BABE RUTH

INDUCTED IN 1939

MUHAMMAD ALI, MICHAEL Jordan — each of these men is a superstar who transcends athletics. But perhaps neither would have achieved such status if it weren't for America's first sports megastar: Babe Ruth.

George Herman Ruth was born in a rough Baltimore neighborhood and sent to St. Mary's Industrial School for Boys — a reformatory and orphanage — at age 7. His ability to overcome difficult circumstances and eventually rise to Big League fame epitomized the American Dream.

While many athletes over the years have earned the right to call themselves stars, only a handful can boast that they've revolutionized their sport. And perhaps no one managed to change his sport as much as the man who would become known as the "Sultan of Swat," the "Bambino" or simply "The Babe."

While other hitters during the early 20th century concentrated on putting the ball in play and on the placement of their hits, Ruth — who also starred on the mound early in his career — was the first man to truly swing for the fences, often out-homering entire teams during his prime years in the Bigs. As recognizable with a cigar in his mouth as with a bat in his hands, Ruth's larger-than-life personality suited New York City perfectly. Sure enough, fans took notice, flocking to the Polo Grounds — and later Yankee Stadium — when he joined the Yankees in 1920. And more than 75 years after his final season, Ruth's star still shines as brightly as ever.

Programs: Home and Away

WITH MORE THAN 1,000 ON-SITE PROGRAMS SCHEDULED PER YEAR, the National Baseball Hall of Fame and Museum often surprises visitors with one-of-a-kind experiences that they may not have been expecting.

Whether it's attending an *Artifact Spotlight* presentation, hearing a Hall of Famer being interviewed about his career, or listening to an author talk about his latest book, there's always a chance of catching a program that blends the Museum's exhibits with the institution's educational mission.

"What we try to do with our public programs is add an element that's entertaining but that's also educational," says Brad Horn, senior director of communications and education. "We focus our programs on audiences composed of both adults and children that allow for an exchange of information."

While the Hall of Fame offers a number of events throughout the year, it's during the summer months that the schedule of daily programming is busiest. Among the recent program highlights are *Baseball Coast to Coast*, a virtual tour of ballparks in the Hall of Fame's *Sacred Ground* exhibit; *Going, Going, Gone!*, where patrons recreate a radio broadcast of a famous home run call; *Artifact Spotlight*, a behind-the-story look at artifacts or exhibits; and *So You Think You Know Baseball?*, where three sets of contestants try to successfully answer nine "innings" of questions.

Other popular events held in recent years include an author series; a *Legends Series* featuring various Hall of Famers; a *Voices of the Game* series with radio and television broadcasters; the Special Abilities Weekend; *A Bridge to Brooklyn*, highlighting the Dodgers' 1955 World Series title; and glimpses of several baseball-themed movies such as *Mr. 3000* and *Everyone's Hero*.

The Hall of Fame also has expanded its reach to other institutions around the country, debuting its first traveling exhibition, *Baseball As America*, at the American Museum of Natural History in New York City in 2002. Featuring more than 500 items from the Hall's collection — including dirt from Brooklyn's Ebbets Field and the farewell trophy given to Lou Gehrig by his teammates — the touring exhibit concluded a seven-year, 15-city national tour in 2008 that drew nearly 2.5 million visitors.

"This exhibition was one of the most successful endeavors in the Museum's history," says Hall of Fame President Jeff Idelson. "At the core of our mission is making our collections accessible to as wide an audience as possible. In touring *Baseball As America*, we accomplished that and know that we only whet the appetites of baseball fans in 15 great baseball cities around America who now want to visit Cooperstown."

MLB All-Star FanFest

THE NATIONAL BASEBALL HALL OF FAME AND MUSEUM BRINGS a little bit of Cooperstown to each All-Star Game. The Hall of Fame has staged an exhibit at the multimedia hardball exposition known as MLB All-Star FanFest since 1991, when the Midsummer Classic was played in Toronto. Recently celebrating its 20th anniversary, the five-day event, which ends on the day of the big game, is held in the host city of each year's contest. And whether or not they'll be attending the game, fans revel in the festivities.

The largest fan-driven baseball event in the world, MLB All-Star FanFest features skills clinics, interactive games and autograph signings, some from Hall-of-Fame players. The Hall of Fame exhibit includes a *Jeopardy!*-like baseball trivia game that is played every hour and has proven a fan-favorite over the years.

"We try to tailor it to the city," says Senior Director of Exhibits and Collections Erik Strohl. "There are things in the exhibit that are for the baseball aficionado that maybe the casual fan hasn't heard of, but certainly items from modern day, too, where kids coming to the exhibit will see names like Albert Pujols, Wade Boggs, Cal Ripken — that are familiar today.

"If you're coming to FanFest and you say, 'Well, I've already been to Cooperstown, so I want to focus on something else,' you really need to come to the exhibit, because you will get to see a lot of stuff that doesn't go on display much."

The short-term exhibit — one of more than 40 attractions at FanFest — has about 100 items from the Hall's collection on display.

Among the items that the Hall of Fame typically likes to show off during All-Star FanFest are jerseys from Christy Mathewson, Dizzy Dean and Jackie Robinson, caps from Lou Gehrig, Duke Snider and Jim Palmer — the one he wore in 1969 when he no-hit the Oakland A's — and bats from Babe Ruth, Ted Williams and Carl Yastrzemski. Nolan Ryan's shoes and the bat that Ted Williams used to collect his 2,000th hit also have made appearances.

"We're very serious about security and making sure that things are transported and displayed in a way that assures they will be protected," Strohl says. "It's our job to care for these things for all of posterity, and we take it very seriously.

"FanFest has become the event of the year for baseball fans. This is a great opportunity to bring part of the Hall of Fame to the people."

Publications

MUCH LIKE A MAJOR LEAGUE CLUB, THE NATIONAL BASEBALL Hall of Fame and Museum publishes a yearbook and magazine, both of which highlight its legendary roster in unique ways. The annual yearbook typically offers short biographies of all enshrinees, in-depth feature articles on new electees, a recap of the rules for election, Hall of Famer statistics, a review of the Ford C. Frick and J.G. Taylor Spink award winners, a list of the Hall's Board of Directors, and numerous feature stories related to both the game's history and its relationship to the Cooperstown institution.

"For many years the yearbook has represented the excellence associated with the Hall of Fame and pays tribute to all Hall of Fame members," says the Hall's Senior Director of Communications and Education Brad Horn, who serves as executive editor of the yearbook. "It remains very popular among our visitors."

More than 60,000 copies of the yearbook are published annually and sold in the Museum and at select outlets. *Memories and Dreams*, the Hall's official magazine, is a premium that is sent to the 30,000-plus participants in the Hall of Fame's membership program. It features original content from Cooperstown and is also available for purchase at the Museum.

"*Memories and Dreams* has grown from a newsletter in 2002 to a 32-page magazine first published quarterly in 2005 and now six times a year," says Horn. "It allows members to go a little bit further inside our content.

"We focus on themes relevant to our Museum mission, any sort of topical theme or something that's relevant to baseball today. The frequency of the magazine allows our members to feel connected to Cooperstown all year round, while the content gives them a meaningful connection to stay in touch with the Hall of Fame."

Cooperstown Symposium

THEY COME BECAUSE OF THEIR LOVE OF BASEBALL; THEY LEAVE with an enriched knowledge of the game. For more than two decades, people from around the country have converged on the National Baseball Hall of Fame and Museum for three days in early June to attend the annual Cooperstown Symposium on Baseball and American Culture.

Held in the Grandstand Theater, Bullpen Theater and Education Gallery, the 2010 edition featured more than 50 presentations on such wide-ranging topics as women who write baseball and baseball in cinema and theater, including a documentary entitled *Ghandi at the Bat*.

Hall of Fame Librarian Jim Gates, a co-coordinator of the event, said that the 160 attendees in 2009, arriving from such far away locales as Australia and Hawaii, surpassed the previous high-water mark by nearly two dozen.

As his three long days were coming to an end in 2009, Gates half-jokingly said he came up with a new advertising slogan: "This is the ultimate baseball geek fest."

While most of the participants came from academia, there were also two judges; a dentist; former Big League first baseman Dan Ardell — who played seven games for the 1961 Los Angeles Angels; and Hugh Hewitt, who broadcast his nationally syndicated radio show from the atrium in the Hall of Fame Library for two nights.

Bill Simons, the symposium's other co-coordinator and a history professor at the State University of New York College at Oneonta, has participated in each of the 21 symposiums and believes that the 2009 event was the best of them all.

"We have some incredible people gather here from a variety of disciplines, and there is a special dimension that you feel," Simons says. "We have become a symposium that welcomes new scopes of people and that adds a tremendous vitality. I think that's reflected in the quality of the presentations.

"We have built up a great history, and that history continues and goes forward," he adds. "This is the preeminent academic baseball conference."

Noted authors Roger Kahn, George Plimpton and Elliot Asinof have been keynote speakers at the symposium through the years, as have documentary filmmaker Ken Burns and former MLB Players Association Executive Director Donald Fehr. In 2009, the honor belonged to Paul Dickson, who spoke about his recently rereleased *Dickson Baseball Dictionary*.

"It has just been absolutely beyond my expectations," says Dickson, who has published 55 books, including eight about baseball, several of which are housed in the Hall's library. "There's a great sense of camaraderie here. As a non-scholar, as a straight-up writer, I go to some scholarly events and you are always considered the outsider, but here it's just the opposite. They don't check your Ph.D. at the door to make sure you're part of the club. It's a very welcoming, wonderful environment.

"Coming in I thought it would be a little dryer. I didn't realize there was going to be such vitality and spirit."

Following spread: Fans at the 2010 MLB All-Star FanFest historic baseball exhibit in Anaheim, Calif.

"AS I REFLECT BACK AND AT THE SAME TIME LOOK AT THE PRESENT AND THE FUTURE, ONE THING IS CERTAINLY TRUE: LIFE DOES NOT OFTEN PROVIDE OPPORTUNITY FOR A PERSON TO MAKE A CLEAN CHOICE. BEING INDUCTED INTO THE BASEBALL HALL OF FAME HAS ALLOWED ME TO TAKE THE LOW POINTS OF MY CAREER AND TURN THEM INTO THE HIGH POINTS OF A LIFETIME. MY INDUCTION ALSO HAS ALLOWED ME TO CREATE A NEW PERSONAL FORMAT FOR MYSELF AND NOW I FEEL PROUD TO TAKE MY SEAT AMONG THE GREATEST EVER TO PLAY MAJOR LEAGUE BASEBALL."

LOU BROCK, JULY 28, 1985

INDUCTION
SPEECH

WILLIE MAYS

INDUCTED IN 1979

At his peak in the mid-1950s, Willie Mays was arguably the best at each of the five essential baseball tools: hitting for average, hitting for power, running, fielding and throwing. It's difficult to imagine a player who could come close to matching that.

Mays didn't just get by on natural talent; he perfected his game far away from the spotlight during a three-year apprenticeship in the Negro Leagues. The son of a well-known semipro player, Mays grew up in Birmingham, Ala., and joined the Black Barons of the Negro Leagues while still in high school. By the time he entered the Giants' farm system in 1950, he was already a complete player. During his rookie year with the Giants, Mays developed a reputation for forgetting his teammates' names. Instead, he used a playful "Say Hey" to greet them. Soon, New York sportswriter Barney Kremenko dubbed him the "Say Hey Kid."

Throughout the 1950s and early '60s, as he grew into baseball maturity, the "Kid" was the darling of baseball fans far and wide. He won his first MVP Award in 1954, following a .345/41/110 campaign, and capped the season with his legendary over-the-shoulder grab in the World Series. He would go on to win 12 Gold Gloves (the prize was first awarded in 1957), hit 660 homers and swipe four stolen-base titles. As one writer once noted after Mays smashed a long extra-base hit: "The only man who could have caught it, hit it."

Gold Glove outfielder Torii Hunter grew up far from Ebbets Field — where Jackie Robinson broke speed and color barriers — listening to his grandfather's tales of the pioneer. But it didn't matter that Hunter never saw Robinson don a uniform or that he never watched the Dodgers star take the field. The Hall of Fame brought them together. Hunter visited the Hall as a Big Leaguer for a glimpse of Robinson's No. 42 jersey — the artifact that transcends generations.

"When I saw the jersey that he wore, I said to myself, 'His skin touched this jersey,'" Hunter says of the man who paved the way for his and countless other ballplayers' careers. "That's the closest I'm ever going to get to Jackie Robinson, and it's all because of the Hall of Fame. When I read about him or see him on TV, it's different than having his actual game-worn jersey right there in front of you. You can't believe you're this close to something he actually touched. He's never touched my book, he's never touched my TV, but he touched this jersey."

Film Festival

MELDING TWO OF AMERICA'S FAVORITE PASTIMES, THE ANNUAL Baseball Film Festival has been a fall tradition at the National Baseball Hall of Fame and Museum since 2006.

Spread out over three days, the festival brings together filmmakers and film buffs from around the country. Approximately a dozen films with varied connections to baseball that have been released within five years of the festival and that range in length from 12 minutes to two hours are shown throughout the day at the Hall's Bullpen Theater. The film festival gives baseball-themed projects an outlet in Museum audiences, while the Museum has partnered the Baseball Film Festival to pay tribute to iconic Hollywood productions incorporating baseball, such as *A League of Their Own* and *Bull Durham* in recent years.

In 2009, *The Lost Son of Havana* and *El Play* were hits with fans. Another gem from the 2009 edition of the festival was *Signs of the Time*. The MLB.com documentary *Base Ball Discovered* was a standout in 2008, while *Rooters: The Birth of Red Sox Nation*, garnered raves at the second annual festival in 2007.

Nationally syndicated film critic Jeffrey Lyons, a judge during the festival's first three years when films competed for awards, said, "The films fill important voids in baseball history. It's one of the reasons I think it's a very important film festival."

The Lost Son of Havana documented former pitching star Luis Tiant's emotional return to his home in Cuba after 46 years in exile. *Signs of the Time* examined the complicated history of hand signals in baseball. *El Play* told the story of an aspiring Dominican player from the baseball hotbed of San Pedro de Macoris, known to scouts as "the cradle of shortstops," and his struggles as he chases his dream of becoming a professional.

"It has been an incredible honor to make a film about one of baseball's legends and to screen it in Cooperstown at the Baseball Film Festival," said Kris Meyer, a producer of *The Lost Son of Havana*.

"To receive an award for baseball excellence from Cooperstown is a real honor, especially when you make a baseball film," said *Signs of the Time* director Don Casper. "Being here for three days, seeing the quality of films that we were up against, it makes it even more special because there were really a lot of great films here."

"It is a great film festival because of the strength and diversity of the films," said Stephen Light, the Hall's manager of museum programs. "It just shows the strength of baseball as a film topic."

The Hall of Fame Game

THE HALL OF FAME GAME MAY BE GONE, BUT IT'S NOT FORGOTTEN. Although the Hall of Fame Classic replaced the exhibition in 2009, the longstanding Hall of Fame Game between actual Major League teams was a special treat in the village of Cooperstown for decades.

The seeds of the Hall of Fame Game were planted in 1939 amid a summer-long celebration of the game's centennial, which featured an all-star game of Major Leaguers and exhibition games pitting the New York Yankees against the Newark Bears and the Philadelphia Athletics against the Penn Athletic Club. On May 30, 1940, *The Sporting News* advocated for such contests to be played annually and suggested that any proceeds benefit the Museum. The self proclaimed "Base Ball Paper of the World" pointed out that the only sources of income for the shrine were the small admission fee paid by visitors and the profit on the sale of souvenirs. The Chicago Cubs and Boston Red Sox returned to Cooperstown in 1940 to inaugurate a beloved tradition. Ted Williams hit two home runs that day, but the Cubs won a wild 10-9 decision.

An article from a Cooperstown newspaper stated, "the Cubs–Red Sox game will be the first step in the proposal to have exhibition contests here annually between teams in O.B. (organized baseball), the proceeds from which will be used in helping maintain the national shrine."

At the annual joint meeting of the National and American leagues, on Dec. 11, 1940, with Commissioner Kenesaw Mountain Landis presiding, the playing of an annual interleague exhibition game between two Major League teams was made a permanent fixture of the schedule. It was also established that earnings from the event be used for the upkeep of the national shrine.

Thus began what Cooperstown came to know as a rite of summer, a sunny afternoon ballgame played on the former cow pasture where Major Abner Doubleday was once thought to have laid out the first diamond and formulated the first rules of the nation's pastime way back in 1839.

Throughout the Hall of Fame Game's illustrious history, a who's-who of Major League stars eagerly made the trip to Cooperstown to participate. The greats who homered in the game through the years included Duke Snider, Mickey Mantle, Bill Mazeroski, Hank Aaron, Orlando Cepeda, Ernie Banks, Carlton Fisk, Willie Stargell and George Brett.

"We don't look at playing in the game as taxing," said then–Arizona Diamondbacks Manager Buck Showalter in 2000. "It's an honor, and our players are excited about coming here."

The Hall of Fame Classic

A NEW TRADITION WAS BORN IN COOPERSTOWN IN 2009 WHEN THE inaugural Baseball Hall of Fame Classic replaced the tradition of the Hall of Fame Game. With the co-presentation by the Major League Baseball Players Alumni Association, a game featuring Hall of Famers and other Big League veterans is now played every year at historic Doubleday Field on the Sunday of Father's Day weekend in June.

The first Classic was a seven-inning affair that took place before 7,069 fans on June 21, 2009. The event featured Hall of Famers Bob Feller, Fergie Jenkins, Paul Molitor, Phil Niekro and Brooks Robinson, as well as former Major League stars Bobby Grich, Steve Finley, Kevin Maas, Jim Kaat, Mike Pagliarulo, Lee Smith, Steve Lyons, George Foster and Bill Lee. The 90-year-old Feller stole the show, though, when he started on the mound and led his team to a 5-4 victory.

"We made a deal — he said no bunting and I told him I'd keep line drives out of the middle of the field," said Molitor, who led off the game against Feller with a single to center.

Feller, famed for the speed of his fastball during his 18-year career with the Indians, faced three batters in the inaugural affair. "I didn't clock it because the radar gun wouldn't have accepted it," Feller said afterward. "I threw as hard as ever. The ball, I think, was going about eight or nine miles per hour."

After the inaugural contest, Hall of Fame President Jeff Idelson hailed the game as a success, adding, "We were happy to see everyone having a good time at the ballpark and connecting families as well as celebrating history today on Father's Day. Not until next year's Classic will that much talent be having that much fun on the dirt."

Pagliarulo, whose double drove in the game's winning run, joked that while being on the field brought back a lot of good memories, the performance end of it was a little tough. "Maybe I'll get a jog in once in a while before the next game."

Of the 26 former Big League players who participated in the 2009 Classic, two — Jeff Kent and Mike Timlin — were in the Majors as recently as the previous season. Kent, a slugging second baseman with the Dodgers before his retirement, captured the 2000 National League MVP Award, and Timlin was a stalwart relief pitcher who helped four teams win World Series titles. Both players had also been generous over their playing years about donating milestone artifacts from their careers to the National Baseball Hall of Fame and Museum.

Among other items, Kent has donated the bat he used to hit his 278th homer as a second baseman, breaking Ryne Sandberg's mark. "It's neat that I was a part of history for the 17 years that I played."

Included in the Timlin artifacts in the Museum are the spikes he wore when he made his 1,000th appearance as a pitcher.

"It's an honor just to be asked to have something in there," Timlin said. "I know my career numbers are not going to put me in there with a plaque on the wall, so it's nice to actually have something in there that is part of me."

Among the youngest to participate in the Classic, the newly retired Timlin and Kent enjoyed rubbing elbows with their heroes. The Hall of Fame Classic returned for Father's Day Weekend in 2010, drawing even more fans for its second installment. Kent returned, as well, to defend his title in the pregame hitting contest, but lost to former outfielder Mark Whiten. Feller was also back for the encore performance, serving alongside Hall of Fame Twins slugger Harmon Killebrew as an honorary captain.

"I liked it so much the first time that I came back," said Kent. "Watching Bob Feller start the game last year was amazing. Playing second base and watching him throw the ball all the way to home plate, I thought that was so cool. Getting to see some of the personalities of the older players was probably more amazing than anything else."

Babe Ruth, George Sisler and Walter Johnson at the 1939 all-star exhibition game. Following spreads: Rollie Fingers, Bob Feller and Mark Whiten play in the '09 Classic.

"AS AN ATHLETE, YOU ALWAYS WANT TO ACHIEVE SOMETHING FOR YOURSELF. BUT AS A CATCHER YOU HAVE TO GO BEYOND THAT FOR THE CAUSE. AND I ALWAYS FELT THAT MY DUTY AND RESPONSIBILITY ON THE FIELD WAS TO MY PITCHERS. I KNOW OFFENSE IS AN IMPORTANT PART OF THE GAME. BUT I WOULD DO WHATEVER IT TOOK TO INSTILL THE CONFIDENCE IN MY PITCHING STAFF, AND ENSURE THE FEELING THAT SOMEHOW WE — NOT YOU, NOT ME, BUT WE — COULD GET THROUGH ANY SITUATION."

CARLTON FISK, JULY 23, 2000

INDUCTION
SPEECH

Chapter 8
Connections

Reaching Out

The National Baseball Hall of Fame and Museum's first foray into cyberspace came in January 1995 with the introduction of the institution's first official website. As the role of technology in daily life has increased, the Hall has adapted, too.

The website (baseballhall.org) allows fans to learn about the Hall of Fame and remotely tap into some of the institution's vast resources. With thousands of pages of content and millions of visits per year, the website has allowed fans around the world to have a relationship with the Cooperstown shrine that might otherwise have been impossible.

"Our web presence is important to reaching visitors all around the world, and we try to offer a snapshot of what Cooperstown holds," says Senior Director of Communications and Education Brad Horn. "In future years we'll incorporate a much stronger interactivity between what appears in the Museum and what is available online, so that the experience then becomes one continuum as opposed to visiting the web to then plan your visit to come to Cooperstown. Our vision is to connect those much closer than they are today."

Aside from its website, the Hall of Fame has a blog (baseballhall.mlblogs.com), Twitter account (@BaseballHall) and presence on Facebook (facebook.com/baseballhall) to update fans on the latest in Cooperstown.

"By staying relevant and becoming more meaningful to every audience that wants to learn more about baseball history, we can share the connections that we provide at the Hall," says Horn. "Moving forward we will find ways to continue to be interactive and to meet our fans where they are, so that they can participate in baseball history even from well beyond Cooperstown.

"The blog, Twitter and Facebook sites — our main social media vehicles — are ways for us to connect with fans all across the world."

Living Legends

Enshrinement into the National Baseball Hall of Fame is not the end of the relationship between Cooperstown and its living members. In a multitude of cases, it's simply the prelude to a mutually beneficial lifelong association.

"We maintain very close relationships with all of our Hall of Fame members, and we work together to expand the footprint of baseball history," says Hall of Fame Senior Director of Communications and Education Brad Horn. "There's a very strong commitment on the part of our Hall of Famers to participate in various projects that benefit the Museum.

"Hall of Fame members are the best ambassadors for our mission."

Hall of Famer Ozzie Smith holds the career mark for assists by a shortstop with 8,375. And even though his 19-year career ended in 1996, he's just as enthusiastic to help out as ever, having taken on the role of the Hall of Fame Education Ambassador since he was inducted in 2002.

"As the Hall of Fame's Education Ambassador, it's exciting to reach so many students," Smith said.

Also, the Hall enlists a living inductee to serve as its spokesman for the annual membership program, with the Big League legend's likeness featured on the membership materials, including that year's membership card.

"Hall of Famers love it because they have an expanded profile; fans love it because they have a membership card that bears the image of that spokesman every year," says Horn, "and then we try to feature that spokesperson in our event calendar."

Famous Faces

You just never know who you might bump into when you're visiting the National Baseball Hall of Fame and Museum. The world-famous institution in Cooperstown attracts approximately 300,000 baseball fans annually. As one might expect, it also has attracted its share of famous faces from outside the baseball world throughout the years. If you make the trip, don't be surprised to find yourself face-to-face with a former United States president, an award-winning actor or even a championship basketball coach.

In recent years, those making the pilgrimage to the baseball shrine have included actors Richard Gere, Bill Murray, John Travolta, James Earl Jones and Tim Robbins; actresses Julianne Moore, Kelly Preston and Lynda Carter; directors Rob Reiner, Garry Marshall, Bobby Farrelly and

Actor Richard Gere and son, Homer, watch the Baseball Hall of Fame Induction Ceremony in 2007. Following spread: Cast reunion for the baseball film Bull Durham.

Ron Howard; broadcasters Chris Berman and Tony Kornheiser; musical artists Paul Simon and Branford Marsalis; and former United States Presidents Bill Clinton, George W. Bush and George H.W. Bush.

Reiner's trip was made even more special and emotional when the Hall of Fame's former chief curator, Ted Spencer, personally took him on a tour that included a stop at the Grandstand Theater for the multimedia presentation "The Baseball Experience."

"They give you the history and overview of the game and how it relates to the history of the country and the whole tradition of passing it down from father to son," said Reiner, the director of several hit films, including *When Harry Met Sally*, *The Princess Bride* and *This is Spinal Tap*. "And I'm sitting there with my 12-year-old son and I just started crying. I started crying because my dad had infused this passion for this game in me and I passed it on to my son.

"So I'm sitting there crying and the lights come up and I'm kind of embarrassed and Ted said to me, 'We put this exhibit in a couple of years ago and it was designed to make a grown man cry.' And I said, 'Well, you did it.'"

Big League Class Trip

SOMETIMES EVEN THOSE MOST IMMERSED IN BASEBALL'S DAY-TO-DAY culture — players, coaches and managers — need a trip to the Hall of Fame to put the significance of playing in the Majors in perspective.

Longtime Minnesota Twins skipper Ron Gardenhire opened the eyes of many of his players during one such visit. Although he had twice traveled to Cooperstown to participate in the annual Hall of Fame Game at Doubleday Field, he had never set foot inside the Museum's walls. That was until recently, when Gardenhire returned as a manager, with his ballplayers in tow, for a tour of baseball's history.

"I said, 'I'm in charge and I'm going to see this doggone thing,'" Gardenhire recalls of his first visit to the Hall — a trip that he mandated for the entire team. "I think it's important to be able to experience that as a group. They kept the museum open for us, which was really special. No one else was in there. Too many players don't really know about the history of the game. Some guys, you ask them who Mickey Mantle was and they look at you like they have no clue, and you're like, 'Come on, you've got to know who Mickey Mantle was.' There was a little hemming and hawing at first from some guys who didn't want to go, but once they got in there, their eyes were glued just reading the stuff. I think every one of them enjoyed the living fire out of it because it was really amazing. It's our history. It's what we are. It's what we do."

And Gardenhire was just as awed as his players, especially when handed one of White Sox great Nellie Fox's bats.

"As a little kid, I always got Nellie Fox bats," he says. "They had the big, thick handles with Nellie Fox's signature. At Cooperstown, I finally got a chance to actually feel one of those big, thick things and it was true. I remember holding it and thinking, 'Wow, I used one of these when I was a little kid.' It was really special and really, really cool."

Todd Helton caught the ball that sent Colorado to its first World Series. He had been with the Rockies 11 years and was already the club's leader in hits, runs and RBI. When the 2007 NLCS ended, Helton got down on one knee and raised both arms in joy; it became the signature image of Colorado's fantastic run. By '07, Helton may not have even been the team's best player, but he *was* still its heart and soul. After the NLCS, he was reduced to tears as he recalled the hot streak that delivered Colorado to the Fall Classic. When they woke up on Sept. 18, the Rockies were fourth in the NL West. Left for dead, they won 13 of their last 14 regular-season games to force a one-game playoff for the Wild Card. They won that game in extra innings, then swept through the NLDS and NLCS for a total of 21 wins in 22 games. It was an unprecedented run, and even a World Series loss to Boston couldn't dampen the Rocky Mountain State's baseball fever. A jersey that Helton wore during the Series is on display at the Hall of Fame in honor of the Rockies' historic feat.